SCIENCE 4

FOR YOUNG CATHOLICS

WRITTEN BY
DR. GREGORY TOWNSEND, PH.D.
AND STAFF

SETON PRESS
FRONT ROYAL, VA

Executive Editor: Dr. Mary Kay Clark
Editors: Seton Staff

© 2012-2020 Seton Press
All rights reserved.
Printed in the United States of America

Seton Press
1350 Progress Drive
Front Royal, VA 22630
Phone: (540) 636-9990
Fax: (540) 636-1602

For more information, visit us on the Web at www.SetonPress.com
Contact us by e-mail at info@SetonPress.com

ISBN: 978-1-60704-090-3

Cover: *Healing of the Paralytic at the Pool of Bethesda* by Murillo

Back Cover: *Cathedral of Our Lady*. Antwerp, Belgium.

DEDICATED TO THE SACRED HEART OF JESUS

Study Skills

Fourth Grade, the first grade level above the Primary Grade Levels, is a good year to introduce outlining as a study skill.

You will notice that in this science book, the Table of Contents is a rather detailed outline of each chapter. That outline is repeated at the beginning of each chapter, and we have been careful to use the outline numbering and lettering within the body of the chapters. We believe this will help students to organize the chapter in their minds, and make it easier to study the concepts.

Not all the information is contained in the outlines, but for study purposes, you might want your student to copy the outline in his or her own notebook. Then your student can fill in any information which is important to remember.

The questions at the end of the chapter sections as well as at the end of the chapters should help students to realize what is important to remember, and add those ideas, in key words, to their study outline.

If you go on the internet, you can find further suggestions for Outlining for Fourth Graders. Outlining for understanding concepts, for studying and for preparing for tests, is an essential skill that will be needed in the years to come. We recommend this especially in the areas of science and history.

We hope you and your student enjoy this book.

Science 4 for Young Catholics

Science 4 for Young Catholics

CONTENTS

Science 4 for Young Catholics

Science 4 for Young Catholics

CONTENTS

Introduction

In the beginning of the Bible, in the first book of the Bible, Genesis, in the very first sentence, we read: "In the beginning, God created heaven and earth." The book of Genesis continues to tell the story of Creation. While most of the story of Creation refers to the Earth, some phrases refer to the Sun and the Moon, such as in Chapter 1, verses 14 to 16:

"And God said: Let there be lights made in the firmament of heaven to divide the day and the night, and let them be for signs, and for seasons, and for days and years. To shine in the firmament of heaven, and to give light upon the earth. And it was so done. And God made two great lights: a greater light to rule the day; and a lesser light to rule the night; and the stars."

There are about 300 references in the Bible to heaven and to the heavens. While we usually think of heaven as the place where souls go after bodily death, the plural word, Heavens, usually refers to the Sun, Moon, stars, planets, and so on. In Psalms, we read in Chapter 18, verse 2: "The heavens show forth the glory of God, and the firmament declares the work of His hands." This means that when we look at the Sun, Moon, stars, and planets, we realize that only God, full of power and might, could have created the heavens and all the things we see in the heavens above us.

Nicolaus Copernicus

We know from the Bible that God led the three kings, the Magi, to Jesus when He was born, by means of a special bright star in the sky. The Magi were not simply kings, they were also astronomers who studied the planets and stars, and were aware that a special star was to lead them to the heavenly King. The star stopped over the town where Joseph and Mary were with Jesus, and the three scientist-kings were able to adore Him and give Him gifts.

While we know there were other scientists, called astronomers, who studied the heavenly bodies in the sky, we usually think of the great Catholic scientist, Nicolaus Copernicus, as the "father of modern astronomy."

Nicolaus Copernicus was born in Poland in 1473. He lived about the time Christopher Columbus lived. Nicolaus Copernicus died in 1543, about 50 years after Christopher Columbus sailed for the Americas.

Nicolaus Copernicus is called the founder of modern astronomy because, before him, scientists used to think the sun, planets, and stars revolved around the Earth. Nicolaus Copernicus realized that the Earth and other planets revolved around the sun. He wrote about his scientific discoveries in a book called "The Revolution of the Heavenly Spheres," which he dedicated to the pope at that time, Pope Paul III.

 **Review Exercise**

1. To which Church did Copernicus belong? _____

2. Copernicus is called the _____ of modern astronomy.

3. Before Copernicus, most astronomers believed that the Sun, planets, and stars revolved around the _____.

4. Copernicus' studies taught him that the Earth and planets revolved around the _____.

5. In which book of the Bible can we read about the Creation of the Sun, the Moon, and the stars? _____

6. We read in Psalms that the _____ show forth the glory of God.

7. The Magi were not simply kings, they also were _____.

8. What famous explorer lived at the same time as Copernicus? _____

9. What four things in the sky do we think of when we refer to "the heavens"?

    _____

    _____

10. To which pope did Copernicus dedicate his book about what he discovered in the heavens?

    _____

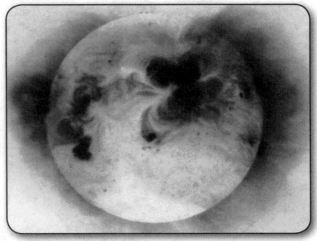

The Sun's outer atmosphere, the corona, can be seen with an x-ray telescope.

Outline of Chapter One

I. The Starry Heavens
- A. The Appearance of the Heavens
- B. The Stars

II. The Universe
- A. The Constellations
- B. The Importance of Stars
- C. Galaxies

III. The Solar System
- A. The Sun
- B. The Planets
- C. Comets
- D. Meteors
- E. Asteroids

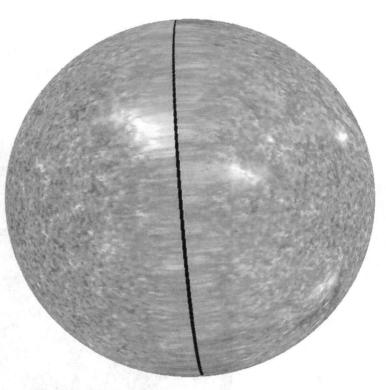

An image of the far side of the Sun based on high resolution STEREO data, taken on February 2, 2011.
Credit: NASA

Chapter Aims

1. know what the heavens look like and know the various objects in it

2. know the definition of astronomy

3. have an idea of what stars are and how far away they are from Earth

4. know what exists in the solar system

5. have an idea of the size of objects in the solar system and the distances between them

6. know what a constellation is

7. know the meaning of galaxy

Activities

1. "star hop" around the Big Dipper

2. observe a star

3. finding constellations

4. find the Andromeda Galaxy

5. explore the size of the solar system

6. explore the orbit of Halley's Comet

7. look for "shooting stars"

8. explore the orbits of the asteroids

I. The Starry Heavens

The scientists who study the heavens are called astronomers. Astronomy is a science that deals with the study of the stars, the planets, and the other heavenly bodies in outer space.

A view from the Hubble Space Telescope
of clusters of stars inside our Milky Way galaxy.
Image Credit: NASA

A. The Appearance of the Heavens

Certain objects in the night sky appear to move on their own across the night sky. The stars and the big bright moon move smoothly through the night sky. The planets seem much smaller. They wander among the stars in a path that changes in speed and direction. We can see comets with their long "tails." Sometimes meteors or "shooting stars" briefly flash across the night sky.

The Big Dipper is the name of a cluster of seven stars that form a shape resembling a big soup spoon or ladle, sometimes called a dipper. This cluster of seven stars is located in a huge group of stars called a constellation. A constellation usually contains several groups of stars that form patterns or designs which are named by astronomers so people can locate them.

The Big Dipper, located in the Ursa Major constellation, is the most useful signpost to star-gazers, as it can be seen throughout the year. From the Big Dipper, we can find our way through the sky to locate other constellations.

Practical Application: "Star Hop" around the Big Dipper: Star Gazing.

To be a good star-gazer, you do not need any special equipment except a book in which you can record the stars and constellations that you see. If you like, make a sketch of each star or constellation you see, and note the date and time. You can use the Sky Log provided on page 7 to record your observations, or you can purchase a little notebook from your local store.

Step 1: When it is dark, go outside and face north. You should soon be able to make out a group of stars shaped like a bowl with a handle. Seven stars make up the Big Dipper: three for the handle and four for the cup.

The two bright stars at the ends are called the Pointers. An imaginary line drawn through them and carried on to the north leads to another bright star called the North Star. This star is almost due north in the sky.

Step 2: Look at the second star in the handle of the Dipper. This star is called Mizar. It is really two stars together. You can see both stars on a clear night. An imaginary line drawn from Mizar through the North Star leads to a W-shaped group of five bright stars. You have "star hopped" to the constellation of Cassiopeia.

Step 3: Follow the line of the handle of the Big Dipper as far again as its length. You will come to a bright, faintly orange star called Arcturus. You have now "star hopped" to the constellation of Bootes, the Herdsman.

When you look at the sky on a clear night to find the Big Dipper, it appears that the Earth is surrounded by a great dome. This dome is called the Heavenly Sphere. If you watch the Big Dipper over a few hours, you will see the Heavenly Sphere rotate about you. It rotates in the same direction that the Sun travels across the sky.

Did the stars seem to be little points of twinkling light that are mounted on the dome, and go round with it? The stars you see near the horizon change from season to season. After a year has passed, you can see the same stars again.

 Review Exercise I. A.

1. _____ is the science that studies the stars and the planets.

2. The people who study astronomy are called _____.

3. The name of the seven stars that appears like a huge soup ladle is called the _____.

4. A huge group of stars that form several clusters is called a _____.

5. What do we call the star that is almost due north in the sky? _____

B. The Stars

The Catholic scientist, Nicolaus Copernicus, helped astronomers explain the way the heavens look. There are stars all around the Earth. There are trillions of stars scattered among the planets. The Earth's rotation, or turning which gives us night and day, causes some of the stars to appear to rise in the east and set in the west. The Earth's revolutions about the Sun cause the changes we see in the patterns of stars during the different months of the year.

The stars, like our sun, are other suns in space. They produce their own light. The stars are different from the planets and the Moon. The planets and the Moon shine by reflecting the light of the Sun, they cannot produce their own light.

Star clusters as observed from the Hubble Space Telescope
Image credit: NASA

Sky Log

Date and Time	Observation (Constellation, Star, Planet, etc.)	Sky Condition	Your Location

Our sun is the nearest star to Earth. It is 93 million miles away. The next nearest star is called Proxima Centauri. If we could travel by car going 65 miles per hour to Proxima Centauri from Earth, it would take us about 50 million years. Light travels much faster than a car, and so it would take only about 4 years for starlight to make such a long journey. However, it takes only eight minutes for our sun's light to make the journey from our sun to the Earth.

Practical Application: "Observe" a Star: Earth's Sun.

The stars are really other suns which produce their own light. Like scientists, you can find out what stars are really like by observing the star closest to the Earth, which is our sun. Our sun is the star nearest to Earth.

The astronomers tell us how to "observe" the Sun by making a pinhole camera.

1. Use a large cardboard box: 12" x 12" x 12" or larger.

2. Cut a ½" hole in the upper part of one end.

3. Tape a piece of aluminum foil over the hole.

4. Poke a hole in the foil with a pin.

5. Tape a sheet of white paper on the inside of the box opposite the pin hole.

6. STAND WITH YOUR BACK TO THE SUN.

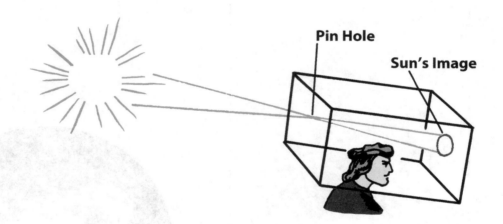

Pin Hole

Sun's Image

7. Hold the box over your head with the pin hole facing toward the Sun.

Other Observations: When you look at the stars at night, do you notice how they seem to "twinkle"? It is really the movement of the Earth's atmosphere that makes them appear to twinkle. "Twinkling" also happens when we look at distant objects on a dry hot day. The planets and moon do not seem to twinkle because they are closer objects in the sky than the stars.

The above illustration shows Earth's rotation in relation to the Sun.

The stars have five basic colors: white, blue-white, yellow, orange, and red. The color of a star depends on its temperature. Have you noticed the color of the charcoal in a barbecue changing as the barbecue gets hotter? White and blue-white stars are the hottest, red stars are the coolest. Our sun is a yellow star. It is neither the hottest kind of star nor the coolest.

Have you ever tried to count the stars? We can see about 2000 stars in the evening sky. Astronomers can see many more stars with their telescopes. These far-away stars are normally too faint to see.

The stars in their great numbers and variety show the mighty and infinite power of God. The stars obey scientific laws made by God; this shows God's Divine Intelligence. Astronomers are only beginning to discover these laws about stars. There are many mysteries in the universe which scientists cannot explain. Only God knows everything about the stars. How wonderful it is that He is our loving Father who nightly presents to us the beautiful stars!

When you look up into the night sky, do you think of God's promise to Abraham? Read in the Bible Genesis 22:17.

Review Exercise I. B.

1. The stars are found all around the _____.

2. The Earth's rotation causes the stars to appear to _____ across the sky.

3. The planets and moon shine because they reflect the light of the _____.

4. The stars shine because they _____ their own light.

5. The movement of the Earth's atmosphere causes the stars to _____.

6. The star called Proxima Centauri is the nearest star to Earth after the _____.

7. The five basic colors of the stars are: white, blue-white, yellow, _____, and red.

8. We can see about _____ stars in the evening sky from any one place.

9. We must use a _____ camera to "observe" the Sun.

10. The color of a star depends on its _____.

An image of a star cluster taken from one of NASA's Explorer satellites
Image credit: NASA/JPL-Caltech/Univ. of Virginia

II. The Universe

When we speak of the Universe, we speak of everything that exists, including all physical matter and energy, the planets, stars, galaxies, and space, all of which are governed by God's physical laws.

A. The Constellations

A constellation is a large group of stars that form patterns or figures or designs. In order to make it easier to describe where a heavenly body was located, ancient astronomers divided the stars into groups. These groups were named after legendary heroes, animals, and objects. People long ago imagined seeing pictures of these people or things when they looked at these groups of stars in the night sky. These groups of stars are called constellations.

Astronomers today continue to use these ancient names for the constellations. They use the constellations to make it easier to describe where heavenly bodies are located and to help find them when gazing at the heavens. This does not mean we believe in any legendary heroes.

 Practical Application 1: Finding constellations.

*Note that the following "sky map" illustrations have the directions of east and west reversed. This is because they are supposed to be viewed while holding the book above your head with the page facing downwards for you to see and apply to the heavens above.

Step 1: When it is dark, at about 10 p.m. in January or 8 p.m. in February, go outside and look toward the south. There you will see the seven bright stars that make up the constellation of Orion. The bright, faintly orange-red star near the top left is Betelgeuse. At the bottom right corner is the white star Rigel. The three stars in a line in the middle make up Orion's belt.

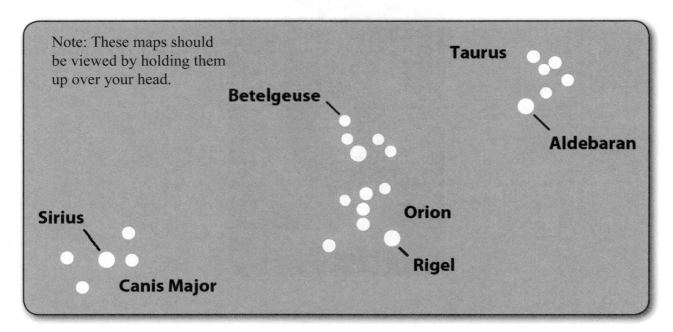

Note: These maps should be viewed by holding them up over your head.

Taurus

Betelgeuse

Aldebaran

Sirius

Orion

Rigel

Canis Major

Step 2: Imagine a line drawn through Orion's belt and follow it upward. It leads to an orange star, called Aldebaran. You have "star-hopped" to the constellation of Taurus, the Bull. If you follow this imaginary line in the opposite direction, it will lead to Sirius, the brightest star in the night sky. You have now "star-hopped" to the constellation of Canis Major, the Great Dog. Sirius is sometimes called the Dog Star.

(You do not need to remember the names of these stars and constellations.)

Looking from Earth, the planets generally move along a path in the heavens, called an ecliptic path. This is an unusual word, pronounced like "ee-clip-tik." Take a dinner plate and slide your finger around in a circle on the plate. The way in which your finger moves around the top surface of the plate is similar to how the Earth and the planets move in the heavens. The planets all move in the same "plane," as if they were on a flat or level "surface" just like the surface of the plate.

However, the planets don't all move in a perfect circle, nor do they move in the exact same shape or pattern of circular orbit around the Sun. The Earth moves in an oblong (elongated) type of circle. The shape of Earth's orbit is said to be elliptical, like a circle that is somewhat flattened and made longer.

Throughout the year, different constellations occupy Earth's region of the heavens, which certainly makes watching the stars in the sky particularly interesting any time of year.

Because Earth is in different places during its yearly orbit or revolutions around the Sun, different constellations are seen from planet Earth at different times of the year. The charts shown on the next pages are examples of the major constellations we see during each of the four seasons.

The Blessed Virgin Mary By Diego Velazquez

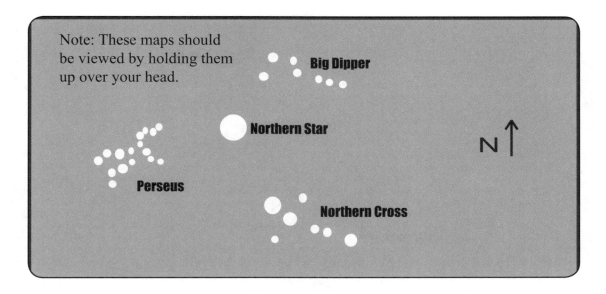

Practical Application 2: The Fall Constellation (9:00 PM)

Step 1. Follow the pointers of the Big Dipper to the North Star. Then look toward the east. In the east is a large group of bright stars. This is the constellation of Perseus.

Step 2. Drop down almost south from the North Star, a little to the west. See the form of a cross made of stars with a bright star at its top. This is the constellation of the Northern Cross or Cygnus, the Swan. Some call it the Kite.

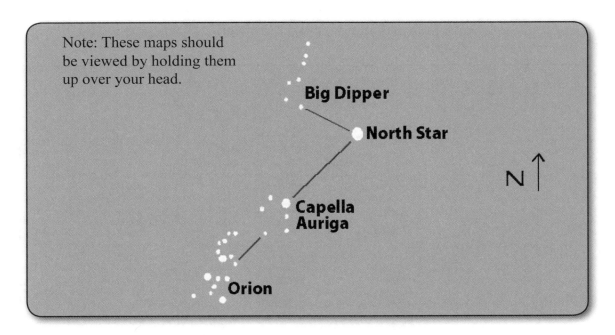

Practical Application 3: The Winter Constellation (9:00 PM)

Step 1. Follow the Big Dipper to the North Star. Then drop south and west to the biggest and loveliest constellation in the sky: the constellation of Orion.

Step 2. About halfway between Orion and the North Star, you will see the constellation of Auriga, or the Charioteer. In it is Capella, the brightest star near the North Star.

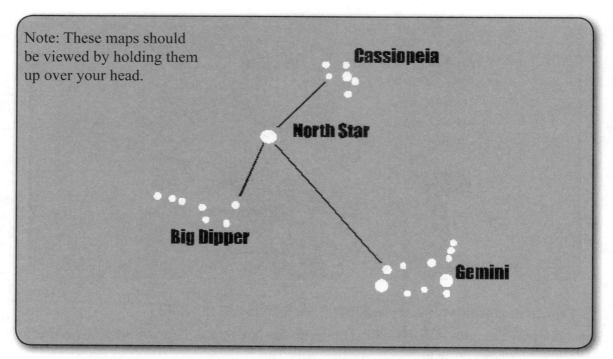

Practical Application 4: The Spring Constellation (9:00 PM)

Step 1. First, locate the Big Dipper. Follow its pointer to the Pole Star. Continue to the west, where you will see a little "W". This is the constellation Cassiopeia (named after a Greek queen).

Step 2. Southwest from this star you will see the two very bright stars, Castor and Pollux (legendary twin brothers). These are in the constellation of Gemini.

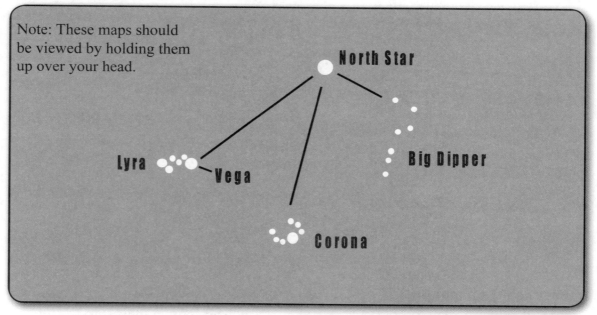

Practical Application 5: The Summer Constellation (9:00 PM)

Step 1. Follow the open bowl of the Big Dipper a little southeast until you come to a very bright star called Vega, in the constellation of Lyra (the Harp).

Step 2. Drop down from the North Star almost directly south and you will see a little round diamond-like brooch of stars. This is the constellation of Corona, or the Crown.

B. The Importance of Stars

God created the stars not only to show us His great power and intelligence but also to help us in different ways in our daily life.

1. Stars as Signs

With the North Star, God has given us a means of knowing our direction. It is a bright star that one finds always in the same place. It is almost right above the North Pole of the Earth. When we face the North Star, we know that we face north; behind us is the south; to the left is the west and to the right is the east. Do you know how to find the North Star? First look for the Big Dipper. If you follow the line from the pointer stars of the bowl of the Big Dipper, they will lead to the North Star. If one lives in the Southern Hemisphere, then one can use the Southern Cross to find the South Pole of the Earth.

Do you remember how the Wise Men found the Savior of the World by using the stars as a compass?

2. Stars as Time-keepers

For hundreds of years, men have studied the stars. They noticed that at different times of the year, they saw different constellations. They gradually realized that it takes about three months for one set of constellations to change position with another. By watching the stars and the phases of the Moon, they were able to plan and develop a calendar.

The calendar we use today starts with the year in which Our Lord was born. That is why we use the initials A.D. A.D. stands for the Latin words Anno Domini, which translated means "In the year of Our Lord."

 Review Exercise II. A. & B.

1. A constellation is a _____ of stars that form patterns.

2. Constellations were named because people imagined they saw _____ of people or things when they looked at them.

3. Constellations are useful to astronomers to describe _____ heavenly bodies are located and to help find them.

4. Stars help us in our daily life as _____ and as time-keepers.

5. The biggest and loveliest constellation is _____.

6. Every season, the constellations _____ position.

7. The three wise men, the Magi, followed a _____ to find the place where Jesus was born.

8. The wise men used the stars as a _____.

9. The calendar we use today starts with the _____ of Our Lord's birth.

10. The initials A.D. stand for Anno Domini, which means " in the year of _____."

C. Galaxies

A large group of stars clumped "close" together is called a galaxy. However, the stars within a galaxy are still separated by very very great distances, distances so great that we cannot even imagine such distances. There are many galaxies in the universe, and they are many billions of miles away from each other.

Our sun and its nine planets are part of a galaxy called the Milky Way. The Large Magellanic Cloud Galaxy is the nearest galaxy to our own. It is in the southern sky, so we are not able to see it from the northern hemisphere.

A constellation is an apparent cluster of stars, but we are not sure how close together they are. A galaxy, on the other hand, is a definite cluster of stars that astronomers can determine (in astronomy distances) are close together.

 Practical Application: Find the Andromeda Galaxy.

Step 1: Locate the constellation of Cassiopeia by star-hopping from the Big Dipper.

The sun is the nearest star to the Earth and so can be observed in far more detail than is possible for any other star. It has a variety of surface features. Dark spots come and go; flaming arches of gas leap far out into space; and solar flares may flash brilliantly for a few moments in the active regions. The yellowish surface of the sun is called the photosphere. **Warning: Never look at the sun directly; its brightness can make one go blind!**

Step 2: Follow the left arm of the "W" of Cassiopeia to "star-hop" to the Great Square to the left of Pegasus (the legendary winged horse).

Step 3: You will find the constellation of Andromeda just to the left of the upper left hand corner of the Great Square. Most of the stars we see belong to the Andromeda Galaxy.

Step 4: In the middle of the great galaxy of Andromeda, just barely visible with the naked eye, you may see a small, fuzzy patch of light. This is the most distant object visible to the unaided eye. It has taken the light you see coming from it many years to travel to Earth.

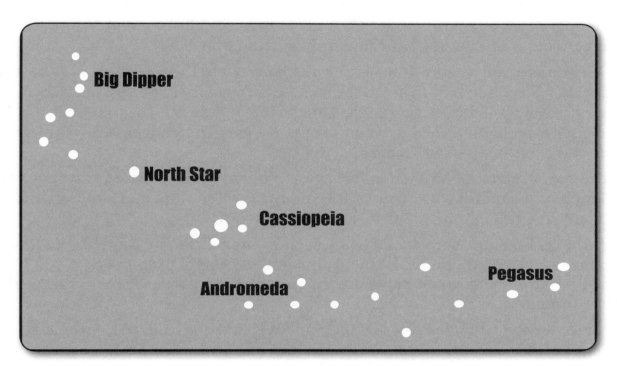

Review II. C.

1. A galaxy is a large group of _____ clumped close together.

2. _____ of miles separate one galaxy from another.

3. Our sun and its nine planets are part of a galaxy called the _____.

4. Most of the stars in the constellation we see belong to the _____ Galaxy.

5. The Large Magellanic Cloud Galaxy is the _____ galaxy to our own Milky Way.

III. The Solar System

The Earth's Sun, together with the planets and all other objects or bodies that orbit around the Sun are called the solar system. The word "solar" means "of the Sun."

A. The Sun

Did you know the Sun is a star similar to the other stars one sees at night? The reason it appears so big is because it is the closest star to our planet Earth.

Compared to other stars, the Sun is of average size, but compared to Earth, it is huge. About a million Earths could fit inside the Sun.

Our sun is a yellow star. It is neither the hottest nor the coolest. However, it is so hot that everything in it is in the form of a gas. You already know that when the temperature of a solid rises very high, it melts into a liquid. If the temperature of a liquid rises even higher, then it evaporates into a gas. The temperature of the Sun is so hot that everything in it is a gas.

The Sun is about 93 million miles away from Earth. If we could travel by car at 65 mph, it would take us about 160 years to travel to the Sun from Earth. Light takes only about 8 minutes to travel the same distance.

Without the Sun, there would be no solar system. The Sun's gravity keeps all the planets circling around it. Without this pull of gravity from the Sun, the Earth and the other planets would move in straight lines away from the Sun rather than circling around it.

Have you ever thanked God for the Sun? Without the Sun, there would be no life on planet Earth. All life on Earth depends on the Sun for food, for warmth, and for light. We need the Sun in a very special way to keep us healthy: sunlight on our skin helps make vitamin D which is necessary for our good health.

God made the Sun also to be His "sign in the heavens." The Sun reminds us that God is the One about Whom we must circle our lives. He is the One who feeds us. He leads us away from the dark world of sin. He lights up the path to Heaven with His grace. Many saints think of the Sun as an image of the Blessed Sacrament and a reminder of the brightest Light of our Faith, Jesus Himself.

 Review Exercise III.A.

1. The Sun is the closest _____ to Earth.

2. One could fit a _____ Earths inside the Sun.

3. As the temperature rises, solids melt into liquids, then liquids evaporate into _____ .

4. The Sun is so hot that everything inside it is a _____.

5. Light takes _____ minutes to travel from the Sun to the Earth; traveling by car would take 160 _____.

6. Without the Sun's gravity, the Earth and other planets would move in a _____ line and not orbit the Sun.

7. All life on Earth depends on the Sun for _____, warmth and light.

8. We depend on the Sun to keep us healthy since it is by means of the Sun that our _____ makes Vitamin D.

B. The Planets

Our solar system has nine planets that we know about. Going out from the Sun, the planets' names are as follows: Mercury, Venus, Earth, Mars, Jupiter, Saturn, Uranus, Neptune, and Pluto [though some astronomers have recently decided that Pluto does not fully qualify as a planet].

Venus, Mars, Mercury and Pluto are made of solid rock and are small planets like the planet Earth. The other four planets, Jupiter, Saturn, Uranus, and Neptune, are giant planets made mostly of gas with a small core of rock and ice. They are much larger than the planet Earth.

Without a telescope, we are able to see four of the planets. They are Venus, Mars, Jupiter, and Saturn. The others are either too small or too far away to be seen without a telescope.

 Practical Application: Explore the size of the Solar System.

Materials: large sheet of paper, string, ruler, pencil, and two thumb tacks

Step 1: Use a large sheet of paper about 24 inches by 20 inches. You can tape several sheets together if needed.

Step 2: Place the sheet of paper on a large board.

Step 3: Make a dot in the center of the paper and push the thumb tacks through the paper about 2 inches each side of the dot, so they are 4 inches apart.

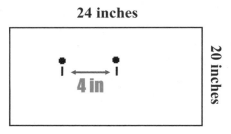

Step 4: Tie the ends of a 20 inch piece of string together to form a loop.

Step 5: Place the loop of string around the pins. Put the point of a pencil inside the loop and gently pull the loop tight. Now move the pencil around the pins keeping the loop tight. It will trace out an ellipse. The oval shape of the orbit of planets, the travel of the planets around the Sun, is called an ellipse.

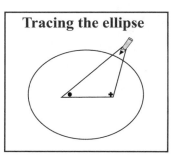

Tracing the ellipse

Step 6: Tie a short piece of string around the loop 3/4 of an inch from one end. Then repeat step 5.

Step 7: Shorten the loop by another 3/4 of an inch and repeat step 5.

Step 8: Repeat step 7, six more times for a total of 9 orbits.

Step 9: Remove the thumb tacks. Draw a small circle between the pin holes. Label this circle "the Sun".

Step 10: Draw a small circle on each ellipse you drew around the Sun. Starting from the inside, label each circle with the name of a planet: Mercury, Venus, Earth, Mars, Jupiter, Saturn, Uranus, Neptune and Pluto.

The Size of the Planets

This picture shows the nine planets drawn to the same scale. The four planets that have orbits nearest the sun are small and made of rock. The next four planets are large and composed primarily of gas. Pluto is solid rock.

The Solar System

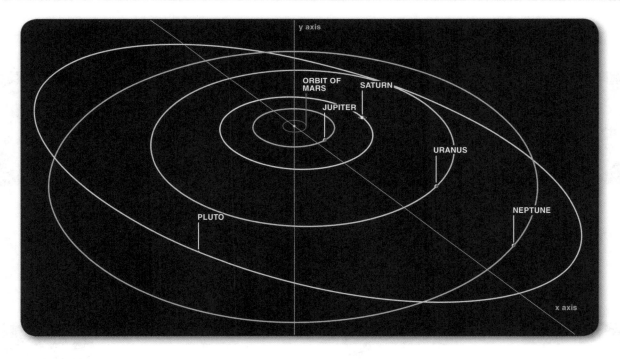

1. The Size of Planets

To get an idea of how the planets differ in size, we can think of the Sun as an object the size of a basketball. In comparison, Earth would be about the size of the eraser on your pencil. Jupiter, the largest planet, would be the size of a ping-pong ball. Pluto, the smallest planet, would be the size of a grain of sand.

2. The Distance Between Planets

To get an idea of the distances between the planets, we can think of putting a basketball representing the Sun at one end of a tennis court. The pencil eraser at the opposite end of the tennis court would be Earth. Nearly two football fields away would be the ping-pong ball representing Jupiter. The grain of sand representing Pluto would be one mile away from the basketball. Between these objects, there is almost nothing in outer space. There are other planets, but they are all smaller than Jupiter. There are also some asteroids, very small rocky-type bodies that orbit around the Sun. To represent the nearest star, we would need to put a basketball 3,600 miles away from our sun-basketball at the end of the tennis court.

The interplanetary missions of unmanned spacecraft have revealed many fascinating things about the planets. The spacecraft have sent back many photographs of the planets and their moons. These photographs reveal even more the beauty in God's creation. They have revealed that all the planets except Mercury and Venus have moons.

The planets remind us of the nine choirs of angels. The angelic choirs are each different and beautiful in their own way. They each circle around God and serve Him in a most loving way.

Mercury   Venus   Earth   Mars

Uranus   Jupiter   Neptune   Pluto

Saturn

Review Exercise III. B.

1. List the nine planets of our solar system. _____,

    _____, _____, _____, _____,

    _____, _____, _____, _____

2. Make up a sentence that will help you to remember the names of the
    planets. A very popular one is: "Many Very Earthly Men Jump Straight Up
    Nearly Perfectly."

    _____

3. What are the giant planets of our solar system?

    _____, _____, _____, _____

4. What planets of the solar system can we see without a telescope?

    _____, _____, _____,

    _____

5. Of what are the planets that are smaller than Earth made?

    _____

A view of the Sun as seen from Pluto

C. Comets

Comets are recognizable by their tails.

Comets are heavenly bodies that resemble giant balls made up of chunks of rock, frozen gases, and ice. The center of a comet is only a few miles in diameter. The tail is a bright mass of colored gas that escapes from the solid center as it heats up. The tail glows because it reflects sunlight and it is very long indeed. Some comets have tails which astronomers believe are millions of miles long! The tail always points away from the Sun. Because of this, the comet is sometimes traveling headfirst and sometimes tail-first in its journey.

However, comets are relatively small in the solar system. Comets are like planets in that they orbit the Sun because of the pull of gravity from the Sun. They are different from the planets in that we see them only once in a great many years. This is because their paths or orbits revolving about the Sun are so far from being circular and take comets far away from the Earth.

We know it takes planet Earth one year to travel around the Sun. The famous Halley's Comet, however, has such a huge orbit so far out from the Sun, that it takes about 76 years to complete its orbit journey around the Sun. Halley's Comet was last seen in 1986. Perhaps you will have a chance to see it when it returns in the year 2062.

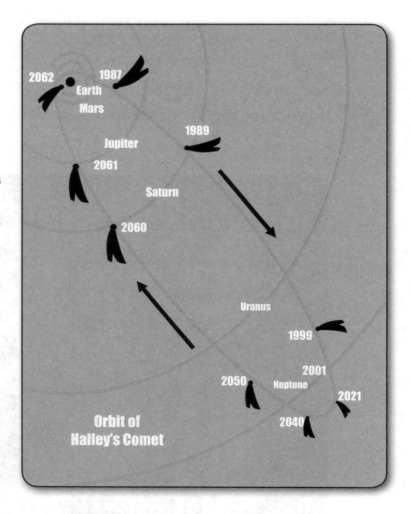

Does the way a comet's tail reflects the Sun remind you of how we should try to mirror God's Image by always turning toward Him?

Practical Application: Explore the Orbit of Halley's Comet.

Materials: diagram of the solar system made in the previous section, string, ruler, pencil and thumb tacks

Step 1: Place your sheet of paper once again on a board.

Step 2: Place a thumb tack in the hole around which you put the circle for the Sun. Take your ruler and measure a length of 2 3/4 inches from the other side of the other hole. Place your second thumb tack at this point. The two tacks are now 6 3/4 inches apart.

Step 3: Tie the ends of a 14 inch piece of string together to form a loop.

Step 4: Place the loop of string around the pins. Put the point of a pencil inside the loop and gently pull the loop tight. Now move the pencil around the pins keeping the loop tight. It will trace out an ellipse.

Step 5: Draw a circle on this new ellipse and label it "Halley's Comet."

 Review Exercise III. C.

1. Comets are like planets in that they _____ the Sun.

2. Comets are different from planets in that we see them only once in a great

   _____ years.

3. The comet has a _____ and a tail.

4. The tail of a comet can be very long indeed and always points _____

   _____ the Sun.

5. Halley's Comet comes into view every 76 years. It will next return in the

   year _____ .

6. We are called by God to _____ His image.

D. Meteors

A meteor is a fast-moving bright object seen for a few moments in the night sky. Meteors are known as "shooting stars" but, of course, they are not stars at all.

Meteors are very small bodies in outer space made of very small bits or chunks of rock or even dust. They could be as small as a grain of sand by the time they land on Earth. Meteors may be pieces of debris that have been thrown off by comets. The friction of the air causes them to become white-hot and to glow brightly. This is why meteors are called "shooting stars."

Sometimes a meteor will be large enough to reach Earth's surface. Most meteors that hit Earth, however, are about the size of a grain of rice! Astronomers believe thousands hit Earth every day! When a meteor hits Earth, it is called a meteorite. When they are very very tiny, the size of a grain of rice, they are called meteoroids. When many appear together, like dust particles in the air, they are called a meteor shower.

Astronomers believe only one or two larger meteors may have collided with Earth in the distant past, and buried themselves in the ground. This is what scientists think happened to form the famous Meteor Crater in Arizona.

 Practical Application: Look for "Shooting Stars."

1. If you look for meteors or "shooting stars" in the night sky, you can see about five to eight an hour. You may need someone to help you recognize them.

2. On some nights, you can see more meteors than usual. These meteors appear to come from one point in the sky. This event is called a meteor shower. It is caused by Earth passing through a swarm of dust-size tiny meteoroids.

3. Meteor showers are named after the constellation from which they seem to have come.

4. Meteor showers are rather common. Look on the internet for any that are predicted to be seen from your location.

5. Look on the internet to find very interesting information about meteors. One website informs us that "Most meteor showers are caused by fragments of old comets scattered along a comet's orbit. When planet Earth passes through a comet's orbit, it sweeps up the fragments, which are heated by friction with the Earth's atmosphere to incandescence, and are visible as bright streaks of light." These meteor showers are usually seen after midnight!

Let us thank God for giving us an atmosphere to protect us from the many meteors that are continually colliding with Earth. The Earth would look like the Moon if God did not give us this heavenly atmospheric umbrella.

On Earth, some meteors come in "storms" or "showers" at predictable times of the year, like the famous Perseid meteor shower in August or the Leonid meteor shower in November.
Credit: NASA

Sin is like a meteorite. It looks bright and shiny for a short while. However, it causes one to fall from God's grace and damages one's soul much worse than a meteorite hitting the Earth. Unlike the damage to the Earth, God in His infinite mercy provided a way to repair the damage to our soul through the Sacrament of Penance or Reconciliation, a spiritual medicine which strengthens as well as heals our soul.

 Review Exercise III. D.

1. Meteors are also called "_____ stars."

2. Meteors are small particles of solid bodies that _____ with the earth.

3. Meteors glow brightly because of the _____ of the air of Earth.

4. A meteorite is a meteor that _____ Earth's surface.

5. Meteor showers are named after the _____ from which they come.

6. _____ causes damage to our souls which only the Sacrament of Penance can heal.

The rings of Saturn can be seen in all their beauty
in this enhanced photo from Voyager.

E. Asteroids

The asteroids are small planet-like rocky bodies that wander between the planets. They are often called "minor planets" because they are so small. They are mostly found between the orbits of Mars and Jupiter in a region called the asteroid belt. A smaller number, however, come closer to the Sun following orbits somewhat like the comets.

If a large enough asteroid crashed into Earth, it could destroy all life on it. The asteroids are so far away from us that we can see them only with a telescope. However, an asteroid called Vesta, found in the asteroid belt, is bright enough to be seen with a sharp eye, appearing as the tiniest point of light in the sky!

 Practical Application: Explore the Orbits of the Asteroids.

Materials: diagram of solar system made in the previous section, string, ruler, pencil and thumb tacks

Step 1: Place your sheet of paper once again on a board.

Step 2: Place a thumb tack in the dot around which you put the circle for the sun. Take your ruler and measure a length of 1/2 inch toward one hole. Place your second thumb tack at this point. The two tacks are now 1/2 inch apart.

Step 3: Tie the ends of a 1 inch piece of string together to form a loop.

Step 4: Place the loop of string around the pins. Put the point of a pencil inside the loop and gently pull the loop tight. Now move the pencil around the pins keeping the loop tight. It will trace out an ellipse.

Step 5: Draw a circle on this new ellipse and label it "Asteroid Ceres." Ceres is the largest asteroid in the asteroid belt.

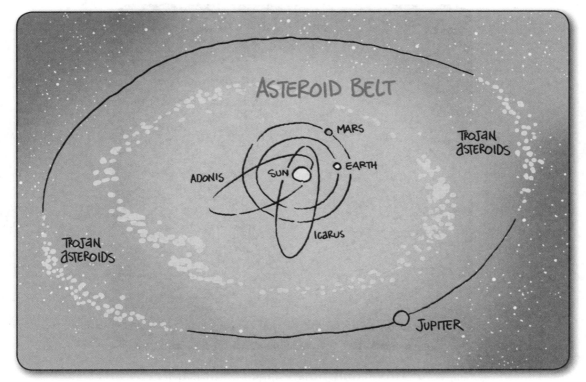

The asteroid orbits crisscross the solar system, although most of them are in the Asteroid Belt between Mars and Jupiter. A few dozen of them, called Trojan Asteroids, follow the orbit of Jupiter.

Review Exercise III. E.

1. Asteroids are small planet-like rocky _____ that wander among the planets.

2. Asteroids also are called _____ planets.

3. Asteroids are mostly found between the orbits of _____

   and _____.

4. The region where asteroids are mostly found is known as the

   _____.

5. Almost all the asteroids are so far away they can be seen only with a

   _____.

6. One asteroid, called _____, is bright enough to be seen with a sharp eye.

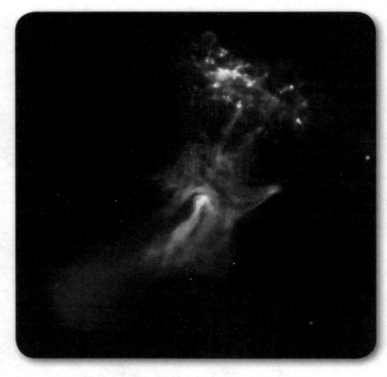

This astonishing image of a pulsar
seems to form an outstretched thumb and fingers,
grasping a burning lump of coal,
much like one might envision of the hand of God.
Image credit: NASA Chandra X-ray Observatory

Review for Chapter One

The Heavens

True or False: Please mark "T" for true or "F" for false.

_____ 1. Our solar system is in the galaxy of the Milky Way.

_____ 2. Comets are balls of gas that come out of the Sun.

_____ 3. All of the planets in the solar system have moons.

_____ 4. Stars are other suns in space, producing their own light.

_____ 5. The beauty and vastness of the heavens show the great power of God.

Please match the words on the left with the correct definitions.

_____ 6. Solar System   a. The science that studies the heavens

_____ 7. Big Dipper   b. Affects the color of a star

_____ 8. astronomy   c. A large group of stars reasonably close to one another

_____ 9. galaxy   d. A constellation that points to the North Star

_____ 10. temperature   e. The Sun and the group of bodies that circle it

Please complete the sentences.

11. A _____ is a group of stars that seem to form a design in the heavens.

12. There are _____ planets that circle the Sun.

13. The biggest planet is _____.

14. The Sun, the nearest star to Earth, is _____ miles away.

15. The force that keeps the planets and other bodies orbiting the Sun is called _____.

Write the name of the nine planets.

16. _____

17. _____

18. _____

19. _____

20. _____

21. _____

22. _____

23. _____

24. _____

Circle the correct answer.

25. Without the Sun there would be no:

    a) solar system b) life on Earth   c) people   d) all of the above

26. "Shooting stars" are:

    a) asteroids   b) meteors   c) comets   d) none of these

27. Without a telescope, how many stars can we see in the evening sky?

    a) 1000 stars   b) 2000 stars

    c) 3000 stars   d) 4000 stars

28. Halley's Comet will return in:

    a) 2000 A.D.   b) 2022 A.D.   c) 2040 A.D.   d) 2062 A.D.

29. Comets are made of rock and _____.

30. The most famous comet is called _____ Comet.

"For thus saith the Lord Who created the heavens, God Himself Who formed the earth and made it, the very Maker thereof: He did not create it in vain: He formed it to be inhabited."

Isaias. 45:2

Introduction

In Chapter One, we studied the constellations, the Sun, the planets, and the meteors, all outside Earth. In this chapter, we will focus on planet Earth, its makeup and about the forces or events which change its surface. We will study the Moon, which orbits Earth and which we can see every day and every night. We will focus on the exploration of the space around Earth. This vast space does not seem to have any boundaries or limits and we have only recently been able to study it in greater detail.

People who lived a long time ago used very primitive scientific instruments. With constant and persistent study of Earth and its Moon, they came to many different conclusions by using logical thinking. Many of these scientists were Catholic or Christian, and certainly through prayer, God helped them to come to correct conclusions.

One great Catholic scientist who studied and learned so much about Earth was Niels Stensen, also known as Nicolas Steno. Niels Stensen was born in 1638 in Copenhagen, Denmark. He lived during the time that St. Isaac Jogues and St. John de Brebeuf were trying to convert the Indians in America.

Niels Stensen used his powers of observation to make important scientific discoveries. During his lifetime, he was recognized as a great scientist and made many original contributions to the science of medicine. Among his chief contributions to science were his explanation of fossils, and his explanation of the geological layers of Earth, which showed how mountains developed. Today, scientists recognize Niels Stensen as the founder of the science of geology, which is the study of the structure of the Earth.

Though Niels was born a Lutheran, he later converted to Catholicism, and was known as a strong practicing Catholic in his parish. Niels said that he owed his conversion to the prayers of an old nun who prayed for him regularly.

Niels Stenson

In his work as a scientist, Niels recognized the wonderful and amazing hand of God, and began studies to become a priest. In 1675, he was ordained a priest and two years later, in 1677, was consecrated a bishop. He spent the last years of his life helping the needy and died in 1686.

Niels was recognized not only as a great scientist, but also as a holy man who was helped by God to discover many scientific truths. In 1987, he was declared "blessed" by Pope John Paul II. Today he is known as Blessed Nicolas Steno.

Mariner 2 explored Venus.

Review Exercise

1. Niels Stensen lived during the _____ hundreds.

2. Niels Stensen made original contributions to the science of _____.

3. Niels Stensen is the founder of the science of _____.

4. Geology is the study of the structure of _____.

5. One of Niels Stensen's chief contributions in geology was his explanation of _____.

6. Niels Stensen explained the _____ layers of Earth.

7. Niels showed how _____ developed.

Outline of Chapter Two

I. The Moon
    A.   Properties of the Moon
    B.   Phases of the Moon
    C.   Eclipses
II. The Study of Outer Space
    A.   The Observation of Space
    B.   The Exploration of Space
III. Planet Earth
    A.   Life on Earth
    B.   Inside the Earth
    C.   The Earth's Crust
IV. The Origin of the Earth
    A.   Forces that Change Earth's Surface
    B.   Earthquakes
    C.   Volcanoes

Chapter Aims

1. know about the Moon and how it affects our lives
2. know about how we explore outer space
3. know about the structure of Earth
4. know the main causes of changes of the surface of Earth

Activities

1. observe the Moon
2. explore why the Moon has phases
3. learn about eclipses
4. use a telescope to observe the Moon
5. discover how a rocket works
6. explore the interior of Earth
7. finding different kinds of rocks
8. explore the detection of earthquakes
9. investigate the eruption of a volcano

I. The Moon

We all know what the Moon is because we see it almost daily in our sky at night. We can see the Moon from Earth because it is the closest and most familiar object in the sky. Sometimes the Moon is fully lit up; other times only part of it is lit up. On dark nights, the Moon provides the light by which we can see. The Moon "shines" in the night sky because it reflects the light of the Sun. The Moon itself has no light. The Sun shines on the Moon just as it does on Earth. Because the Moon reflects some of this sunlight onto Earth, we are able to see this light on the surface of the Moon.

A. Properties of the Moon

We have learned a great deal about the Moon since the invention of telescopes. Telescopes are optical instruments used in astronomy that help us to see objects that are very far away, such as the Moon and other planets.

Telescopes have shown us that the surface of the Moon is made up of smooth plains, jagged mountains, and craters. Even from Earth, with telescopes, we can see some of these features of the Moon. We can see them because there is no atmosphere on the Moon to "cloud" up our view.

The Moon is a very large round planet-like body made up of rocky material that circles the Earth. Earth is fifty times larger than the Moon, which means that fifty moons could fit into the planet Earth. If we compare the size of Earth to the size of the Moon, Earth would be the size of a basketball while the Moon would be the size of a tennis ball.

Because the Moon is so much smaller than Earth, there is less pull of gravity on the Moon than on Earth. The pull of the Moon's gravity is very weak compared to Earth. A person who can jump 3 feet on Earth could jump about 18 feet on the Moon. There is just not enough gravity on the Moon to hold a person as much as the pull of gravity on Earth.

Because of the Moon's low mass, there is less pull of gravity on the moon than on Earth. The Moon's gravity is very weak. The astronauts who landed on the moon could jump high up about 18 feet, compared to about 3 feet on Earth.

The Moon is less than one third the size of Earth. Unlike Earth, the Moon has no atmosphere.

Because the Moon's gravity is so weak, it cannot hold any atmosphere. Since the Moon does not have an atmosphere, the Moon's surface is quite different from the surface of Earth.

For example, there is no wind on the Moon, since wind is a movement of the atmosphere. There are no clouds or weather on the Moon because it lacks any water of its own. There is no air on the Moon. Therefore, there is no sound on the Moon because sounds travel in air. The temperature on the Moon varies greatly. During the day, it can be hot enough to boil water, while during the night it can be cold enough to freeze any gases that may be found on the moon. If there were any oxygen on the Moon like that on Earth, it would freeze.

In European poetry, the Moon is often referred to as "Our Lady's Lantern" because it reflects the Sun's brightness, or glory, just as Our Lady, the Blessed Mother, reflects the glory of God.

 Practical Application: Observe the Moon.

Using the Moon Log on the next page, record your observations of the Moon's appearance twice a week. Make sure you record your observations at the same time of day, and from the same location.

Make sure you notice if:

1. the Moon is in the same place in the sky at the same time every night;

2. the Moon has the same appearance from one night to the next.

Can you answer these two questions?

3. Is there any time during the month when you see the Moon during daylight? _____

4. What is the size of the smallest coin held out at arm's length that covers the Moon in your line of vision? _____

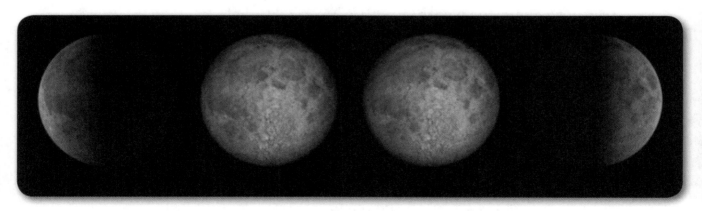

Phases of the Moon

Moon Log

LOCATION OF OBSERVATION SITE: _____

	DATE	MOON COLOR	WEATHER	DRAWING OF MOON'S SHAPE
1.	_____	_____	_____	
2.	_____	_____	_____	
3.	_____	_____	_____	
4.	_____	_____	_____	
5.	_____	_____	_____	
6.	_____	_____	_____	
7.	_____	_____	_____	
8.	_____	_____	_____	

Review Exercise I. A.

1. The Moon circles the _____.

2. _____ moons could fit inside the Earth.

3. The Moon has no _____.

4. There is no wind on the Moon because there is no _____ on it.

5. Are there clouds or weather on the Moon? _____

6. There is no sound on the Moon because there is no _____ on it.

7. The temperature on the Moon _____ greatly.

8. The Moon shines because it reflects the _____ from the Sun.

9. The Moon's gravity is very _____ compared to that of Earth.

10. In Europe, the Moon is often referred to as "Our Lady's _____" because it reflects the Sun's brightness.

B. Phases of the Moon

The Moon reflects some sunlight onto Earth and that is why we see the Moon as being lit up. As the Moon travels in its orbit around Earth, we see different amounts of the Moon's lighted surface. The amount of lighted surface we see are called phases of the Moon. What we call the light of the Moon, which actually does light up a dark night, is the reflection of sunlight from the Moon to Earth.

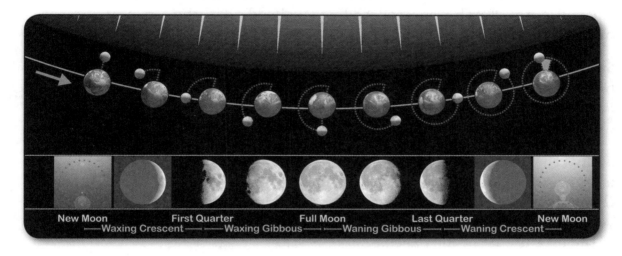

New Moon — Waxing Crescent — First Quarter — Waxing Gibbous — Full Moon — Waning Gibbous — Last Quarter — Waning Crescent — New Moon

The relation of the phases of the Moon with its revolution around Earth.
The sizes of Earth and Moon, and their distance, as seen here, is not to scale.
Image credit: Orion 8

Over a calendar lunar [Moon] month, the Moon makes one complete revolution around the planet Earth. During this time, the Moon passes through all its phases, going from completely dark to completely bright and then back to completely dark again.

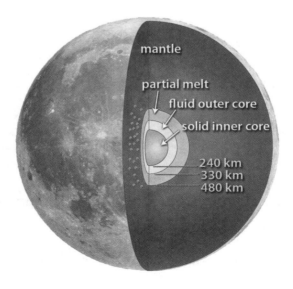

mantle

partial melt
fluid outer core
solid inner core

240 km
330 km
480 km

Layers of the Moon
Image credit: NASA

Practical Application: Explore why the Moon has phases.

Materials: darkened room, electric lamp, and baseball

Step 1: Place the electric lamp on a table in a darkened room.

Step 2: Hold the baseball up over your head in your hand at arm's length with your back to the light. You will see that the phases of the Moon are caused by the changing positions between the Sun (represented by the electric lamp), Earth (represented by your head), and the Moon (represented by the baseball).

Step 3: Raise the baseball enough above your head to allow the light to strike the ball. Note the part of the baseball that is shining bright. This represents the full Moon.

Step 4: Slowly turn yourself around in a counterclockwise direction keeping the baseball in front of you and above your head. Look at how the shape of the bright part of the baseball changes as you make one complete turn. Do you see the phases of the Moon? Your turning imitates the motion of the Moon around Earth once a month.

Slowly rotate counterclockwise while holding the baseball high over your head. Observe how the bright part of the baseball changes. You will see the phases of the Moon.

Step 5: Repeat turning your body and have a friend draw the shape of the bright part of the baseball at the four compass points: north (new Moon), west (first quarter), south (full Moon) and east (last quarter).

 Review Exercise I. B.

1.   The changes in the amount of lighted surface of the Moon which we see are called _____ of the Moon.

2.   The Moon shines in the night sky because it _____ the light of the Sun.

3.   Over a calendar lunar month, the Moon makes one complete _____ around planet Earth.

4.   Over a month, the Moon goes through the phases of New Moon, First Quarter, _____, and Last Quarter.

5. During the revolution, the Moon goes from completely dark to completely
_____ and then back to completely dark.

Phases of the Moon

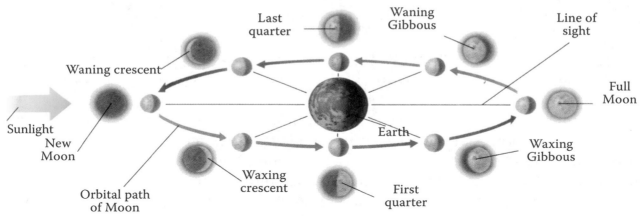

As the Moon travels around Earth, we see different amounts of the Moon's lighted surface. These changes in the amount of lighted surface we see are called the phases of the Moon.

C. Eclipses

As the Sun shines on Earth and the Moon, both throw a long shadow into space. We have night on Earth because every evening, we are carried around by Earth's rotation into Earth's own shadow.

Hold the baseball toward the light at eye level to observe a solar eclipse. Turn to point the baseball away from the light to see a lunar eclipse.

At certain times, the Moon passes between Earth and the Sun in such a way that the people on Earth cannot see the Sun because the Moon is in the way. The shadow of the Moon partially or fully blocks the Sun. This phenomenon is called an "eclipse of the Sun" or solar eclipse.

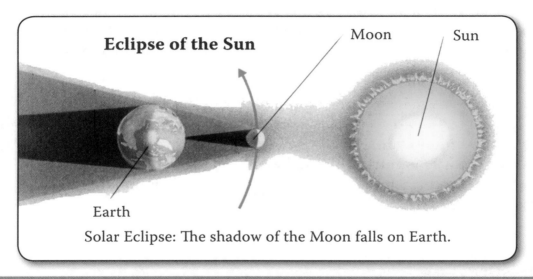

Solar Eclipse: The shadow of the Moon falls on Earth.

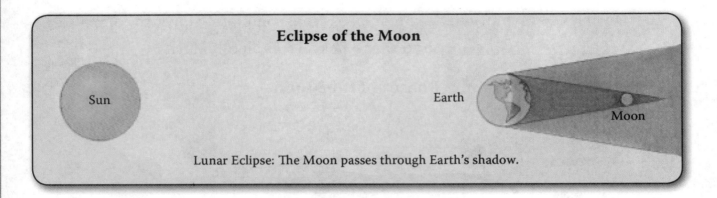

Eclipse of the Moon

Sun

Earth

Moon

Lunar Eclipse: The Moon passes through Earth's shadow.

A partial solar eclipse can occur a minimum of two times a year and up to five times a year. A total solar eclipse occurs about every 18 months, about every year-and-a-half. These eclipses are not seen all around planet Earth, but can be seen only in limited areas of Earth. A total coverage of the Sun lasts only about 6 to 7.5 minutes. If you want to see it, you need to be in the right place at the right time!

A lunar eclipse also occurs. Sometimes Earth passes between the Sun and the Moon in such a way that Earth cuts off the sunlight that the Moon reflects and the Moon cannot be seen at all. This darkening of the full Moon by the shadow of Earth occurs about every six months. This phenomenon is called an "eclipse of the Moon" or lunar eclipse.

An eclipse reminds us of the darkness caused by sin which can cut us off from God, Who is the Sun of our lives. We want to be sure that nothing, no person or thing, cuts us off from the rays of God's grace.

 Practical Application: Learn about eclipses.

Materials: darkened room, electric lamp and baseball

Step 1: Place the electric lamp on a table in a darkened room.

Step 2: Hold the baseball in your hand at eye level with your back to the light as in the illustration. Note that no part of the baseball is shining because the shadow from your head prevents any light from the lamp reaching it. You can see that a lunar eclipse is caused by Earth (represented by your head) coming between the Sun (represented by the electric lamp) and the Moon (represented by the baseball).

Step 3: Hold the baseball in your hand at eye level with your front to the light. Note that you are not able to see the lamp shining because the shadow from the baseball prevents any light from reaching your eyes. You can see that a solar eclipse is caused by the Moon (represented by the baseball) coming between the Sun (represented by the electric lamp) and Earth (represented by your head).

Review Exercise I. C.

1. We have night on planet Earth because we are carried by Earth's rotation into the _____ of Earth.

2. An eclipse of the Sun is when the Moon passes between Earth and the _____.

3. The event above is called a _____ eclipse.

4. An eclipse of the Moon is when Earth passes between the Sun and the _____.

5. The above event is called a _____ eclipse.

6. An eclipse of the Sun lasts about _____ minutes.

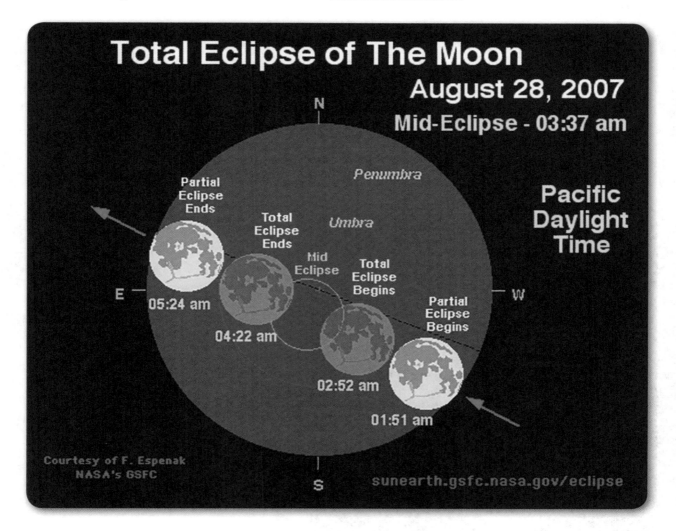

II. The Study of Outer Space

A. The Observation of Space

Without the help of a telescope, we can see about 2000 stars at one time. Scientists have used telescopes and cameras to help them see more very faint stars in the night skies.

 Practical Application: Use a telescope or binoculars to observe the Moon.

Materials: telescope or pair of binoculars

Step 1: Obtain a simple telescope or a pair of binoculars and use them to observe the Moon.

Below you will find a simple photo of the Moon. After using the telescope or binoculars, compare what you see to the photograph of the Moon to see how they differ.

Note that if you are using a telescope, the figure will appear to be upside down.

Step 2: The major features you will find on the Moon are the highlands (which are the light parts of the Moon) and the maria (which are the dark parts of the Moon).

Step 3: You also will find craters, mountain ranges, and winding valleys called rilles.

Apollo 16 camera image
of the Moon's far side.
The lower left part of the image shows a
portion of the Moon visible from Earth.

There are two kinds of telescopes that scientists use.

1. A reflecting telescope uses a large, curved mirror to collect light from a distant star or planet. The image produced by this mirror is looked at with a magnifying glass called an eyepiece.

Refracting Telescope

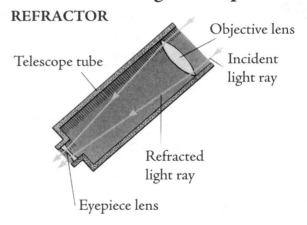

REFRACTOR

Telescope tube

Objective lens

Incident light ray

Refracted light ray

Eyepiece lens

Reflecting Telescope

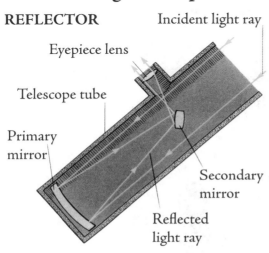

REFLECTOR

Incident light ray

Eyepiece lens

Telescope tube

Primary mirror

Secondary mirror

Reflected light ray

2. A refracting telescope uses a large lens to collect light from stars or planets. The image this lens produces is looked at with a simple magnifying glass called an eyepiece.

The simple telescopes for sale in local stores are examples of refracting telescopes. You can see the large lens at the front of the telescope. The other lens in the eyepiece acts as a simple magnifying glass to examine the image produced by the large lens. Binoculars are simply two refracting telescopes placed side by side.

Astronomers often use a camera attached to the telescope in order to obtain a permanent record of what they see and to produce an image of very faint objects.

The air above planet Earth presents a problem to astronomers when they study the stars. The air makes the stars twinkle and so the stargazer cannot see the stars clearly. Because of this problem, astronomers put their telescopes on high mountains where the air is more clear and still.

For a long time, hundreds of years, astronomers had wanted to be able to view the stars through a telescope placed outside Earth's "cloudy" atmosphere.

In 1990, astronomers, with the help of the National Aeronautics and Space Administration (NASA), placed the Hubble Space Telescope in orbit around planet Earth, outside Earth's atmosphere. Now astronomers are using the Hubble Space Telescope to obtain clearer photographs of the stars and planets found in outer space.

Review Exercise II. A.

1. A refracting telescope uses a large _____ to collect the light from a planet or a star.

2. A reflecting telescope uses a large, curved _____ to collect the light from a planet or a star.

3. The air above Earth makes the stars _____, and so their image cannot be seen clearly.

4. To view the stars clearly, astronomers had wished to place a telescope outside Earth's cloudy _____.

5. The Hubble Space Telescope that was placed in orbit around Earth allows astronomers to obtain _____ photographs of the stars and planets.

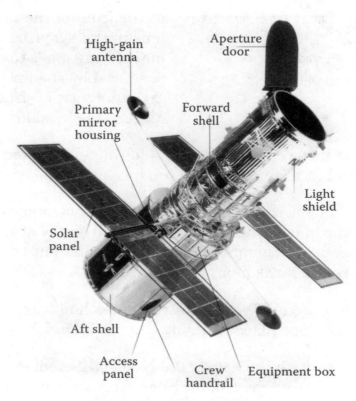

The Hubble Space Telescope

B. The Exploration of Space

Besides viewing the heavens from Earth, men have dreamed about exploring the heavenly bodies. Before they could explore the planets and other bodies in outer space, they had to figure out a way to travel into space. Then they would want to send instruments into outer space that would be able to observe outer space closer up. The instruments would make it possible for them to take photographs and various measurements of space.

Over time, scientists found that the best way to put objects such as satellites into space, was to send a rocket into space. The gases that blast from the exhaust of the rocket give the rocket the tremendous force needed to overcome the strong pull of gravity of the planet Earth. The force can push the rocket at some distance away from the surface of Earth. Today, the satellites that have been carried by the rockets still orbit Earth, taking pictures or measurements. Some of the satellites that have been carried by rockets have traveled even to other planets.

Some satellites have carried men and women with the purpose of exploring outer space. The most important events in the exploration of space have been the following.

The Agena Target Vehicle as seen from the Gemini 8 spacecraft during rendezvous. This was the first time two spacecraft successfully docked, which was a critical milestone if a mission to the Moon was to become a reality.

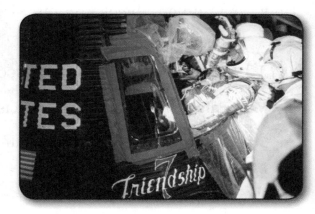

Project Mercury Spacecraft
Crew - one man

- Yuri Gagarin, a Russian from the former Soviet Union, became the first man to orbit Earth in 1961.
- John Glenn became the first American to orbit Earth in 1962, in a *Mercury* Spacecraft.
- Valentina Tereshkova, a Russian woman from the former Soviet Union, became the first woman in space. She orbited the Earth 48 times in 1963.
- Astronauts from the former Soviet Union and the United States were the first to leave their spacecrafts to walk in space in 1965.
- Edward White was the first American to walk in space outside a *Gemini* spacecraft in 1965.

Project Apollo Spacecraft
Crew - 3 men

- Neil Armstrong and Edwin Aldrin, both Americans, were the first men to land on the Moon, on July 20, 1969. They used an *Apollo* spacecraft called *Apollo 11*.
- From 1969 to 1972, the United States landed men on the Moon six times, using different *Apollo* spacecrafts. In all, a total of twelve American men have walked on the Moon. No other country has landed a man on the Moon as of December 2013.
- The space shuttle *Columbia* was launched in 1981. It was the first reusable spacecraft.

Man on the Moon

The launch of the Hubble Space Telescope and the plans to establish a permanent manned space station in orbit around Earth are other exciting events to watch.

Like the rockets and spacecraft that help us move closer to the heavenly bodies, the sacraments help us move closer to God. The more we receive Him in Holy Communion, the clearer our vision of Him will be.

 Practical Application: Discover how a rocket works.

Materials: balloon, milk carton, scissors, tub of water

Step 1: Cut the milk carton in half with the pair of scissors.

Step 2: Cut a small hole in the base of the milk carton.

Step 3: Blow up the balloon and push its neck through the hole in the base of the milk carton. Pinch the neck to prevent the balloon from deflating.

The boat moves across the water propelled by the push of gas expanding from the ballon.

Step 4: Place the milk carton "boat" on the top of the water in the tub and release the neck of the balloon. The "boat" will move across the water propelled by the push of expanding gases from the balloon. This push from expanding gases is how a rocket moves away from the Earth's surface.

This balloon rocket uses the pressure difference between the gas (air blown inside the balloon) to air outside the balloon. The air inside moves quickly towards the outside area of lower pressure.

Review Exercise II. B.

1. Scientists have found that the best way to put objects into space such as satellites is by sending a _____ into space.

2. The blast of gases from the exhaust of the rocket helps to overcome the pull of Earth's _____.

3. _____ was the first man to orbit Earth in 1962 in the first spacecraft called *Mercury*.

4. When did man first land on the Moon? _____ What was the name of that spacecraft? _____

5. Who were the first Americans to step foot on the Moon? _____ and _____

6. As of 2013, how many times have American men landed on the Moon? _____

Edward White-First Space Walker
Image credit: NASA

III. Planet Earth

In this section, we will study planet Earth, the third planet from the Sun. The planet Earth is about 93 million miles away from the Sun. Earth is unique among all the planets of the solar system because, as far as we have discovered, it is the only planet that supports life as we know it.

A. Life on Earth

The planet Earth possesses many qualities which make it possible for humans to live on it.

First, the atmosphere on Earth is perfectly suited for the needs of life as we know it. Some of the higher layers of the atmosphere protect us from dangerous rays coming from the Sun. The atmospheres of other planets, like Mars and Venus, are not suitable for human life.

Second, the orbit of Earth about the Sun gives Earth the ideal temperature range for life as we know it. The daily rotation of Earth about itself also helps keep temperatures cool.

Third, God positioned Earth perfectly within the solar system so that Earth receives the right amount of heat from the Sun. Earth's atmosphere keeps this heat from escaping, which makes the surface of planet Earth comfortable for humans to live.

Fourth, Earth has a strong magnetic field that shields the planet from radiation that is harmful to life. Earth's Magnetic Field allows compasses to work, but most importantly, Earth's magnetic field protects Earth from solar particles which stream out constantly from the Sun. Sometimes these solar particles race toward Earth at incredible speeds. However, these particles are deflected by Earth's magnetic field.

For these reasons and others, planet Earth occupies a unique place among all the planets of the solar system. The discoveries of scientists show us how loving God has been toward us. As we continue our studies, we shall see other features which make our planet special and which highlight God's great love for us. God created Earth for us to live on so that we could know, love, and serve Him on Earth, and then be happy with Him in Heaven.

B. Inside the Earth

Let's study how Earth looks on the inside. The science that deals with the study of the structure of Earth is called geology. The scientists who study the structure of Earth are called geologists.

By studying how earthquakes travel through Earth, geologists have come to believe that Earth is made up of separate layers, just like an onion. Each layer is made of different materials. The four layers of Earth are called the crust, the mantle, the outer core, and the inner core.

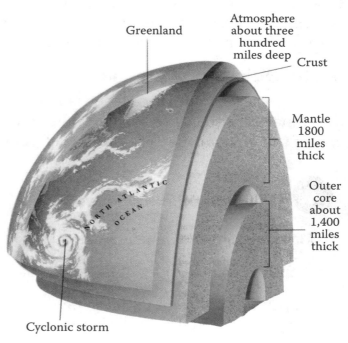

1. The Crust

The crust is a very thin outer layer of rock. Most familiar to us is the material on the surface of this layer: soil, sand, gravel, rocks, as well as the waters of rivers, lakes, and seas. We know that this surface material is not very deep. If we dig a few feet, or at most a few hundred feet, we strike the solid rock in Earth's crust.

The crust of the Earth is much thicker under the continents than under the ocean, but it is still a very thin layer of rock on which we live.

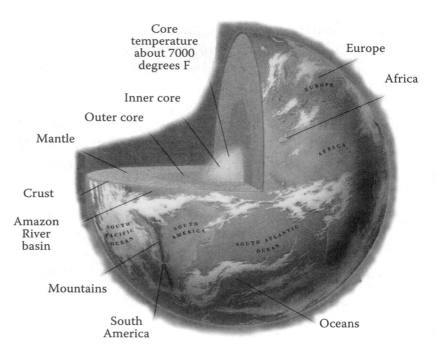

2. The Mantle

Beneath the crust lies the mantle, a zone which goes down about 1800 miles. It is very solid rock because of the tremendous pressures exerted on it. The mantle is made up of rock that is heavier than the rock in Earth's crust but is lighter than the material in the innermost zone, the core.

3. The Outer Core and Inner Core

The outer core or third layer is hotter than the mantle and seems to be liquid. The inner core seems to be solid. The solid inner core is a small sphere about the size of the Moon, thus 1/50 the size of planet Earth.

 Practical Application: Explore the interior of Earth.

Materials: sheet of paper, ruler, compass and 4 crayons

Step 1: Using the ruler, make two dots on the paper that are 10 inches apart.

Step 2: Put the point of the compass on one dot and set the pencil on the other dot you marked. Draw a circle around one of the dots. This circle represents Earth.

Step 3: With the ruler, separate the compass point and the pencil by 2 inches. Put the point of the compass on the dot that represents the center of Earth and draw a circle around it. This circle represents the inner core of Earth. Color it with a yellow crayon.

Step 4: With the ruler, separate the compass point and the pencil by 5 inches. Put the point of the compass on the dot that represents the center of Earth and draw a circle around it. This circle represents the outer core of Earth. Color it with a red crayon.

Step 5: With the ruler, separate the compass point and the pencil by 9½ inches. Put the point of the compass on the dot that represents the center of Earth and draw a circle around it. This circle represents the mantle of Earth. Color it with an orange crayon.

Step 6: The remaining layer circle represents the crust of Earth. Color it with a purple crayon.

Each of the colors represent one of the multiple layers of planet Earth.

> **Notice:**
>
> — how thin the crust of Earth is.
>
> — only the innermost core of Earth is not donut-shaped.

Review Exercise III. B

1. By studying the way _____ travel through planet Earth, geologists believe that the planet Earth is made up of 4 layers.

2. The 4 layers are: the _____, the _____, the outer core, and the inner core.

3. The crust is a very thin _____ which is mostly rock.

4. The mantle goes down about _____ miles.

5. The inner core is a sphere about the size of the _____, 1/50 the size of Earth.

6. The outer part of the core seems to be _____ and the inner part seems to be solid.

C. The Earth's Crust

The solid part of Earth's crust is made up of great masses of hard material called rock. The science that deals with the study of rocks is called petrology. The root *petro-* from Latin means rock or stone. The scientists who study the rocks of Earth are called petrologists. Petrologists classify rocks according to how they seem to have been formed.

In this section, we will learn about three kinds of rocks: igneous rock, sedimentary rock, and metamorphic rock.

1. Igneous Rock.

Some rocks seem to have been formed from the cooling of hot material, such as from volcanoes within Earth's crust. Such rock is called "igneous" (**ig**-nee-us) which means *formed from fire*.

Basalt is a very common type of igneous rock. It is a dark brown, green, gray, or black rock. Granite is another kind of igneous rock which is used today in modern kitchens as a countertop. It is a very large and coarse rock that when cut and polished is frequently used in monuments and buildings.

2. Sedimentary rock.

Sedimentary (sed-de-**men**-ta-ree) rock seems to have been formed by the "cementing" together of materials such as sand, clay, mud, and pebbles that have been deposited by water. Common forms of sedimentary rock are limestone, sandstone, and shale.

3. Metamorphic rock.

Metamorphic (meta-**mor**-fik) rocks have changed shape because of heat and pressure. Marble is a common metamorphic rock formed from limestone by heat and pressure. It is used for marble tiles in floors and bathrooms, and also in monuments and the exterior of buildings.

God created the heavens, the Earth,
and all living things from nothing.

 Practical Application: Finding different kinds of rocks.

Step 1: Collect as many small rocks as you can find in your neighborhood. Write down where you found them.

Step 2: Divide the rocks into the three main groups.

Step 3: After you identify your rocks, divide the rocks in each group into little collections that have the same size, shape, color, and hardness.

Step 4: With your parents' help, try to learn what the rocks tell you about the history of your area. If they are igneous rocks, they would indicate that a volcano erupted sometime in the past. Sedimentary rocks would indicate that a lake or a river existed there sometime in the past. Metamorphic rocks would indicate a movement of Earth's crust, like a fold.

Rocks are made up of one or more of the over 2000 chemical substances that are found naturally in Earth's crust. Such substances as gold, copper, quartz, and rock salt are examples of minerals found in Earth's crust. Petrologists identify the various minerals in a rock by looking at the various properties the minerals have. Such properties as weight, color, hardness, and shape help scientists identify the minerals in a rock.

Remember that St. Peter is the Rock upon which Jesus built His Church. Does the term petrologist remind you of the first pope?

Review Exercise III. C.

1. Igneous rocks are formed from the cooling of _____ material.

2. What are two common forms of igneous rock? _____

3. Sedimentary rocks are formed from the _____ together of various materials.

4. What is a common form of sedimentary rock? _____

5. What made the shape of metamorphic rock? _____

6. What is a common rock formed from limestone? _____

7. What is the science that deals with the study of rocks?
   _____

8. What was the name of the first pope? _____

9. Give two examples of minerals found in Earth's crust?
   _____

10. What are four properties that petrologists use to identify minerals?
    _____

IV. The Origin of the Earth

The beginning of Earth is described to us in the first verses of the Bible. "God created the heavens, the earth and all living things" from nothing, by means of His power.

Scientists have speculated about the origins of the universe and everything within it and have tried to understand the means God used to form the Earth into the way it is today.

"In the beginning, God created heaven and earth" (Genesis Chapter 1, verse 1).

A. Forces that Change Earth's Surface

The studies of scientists have revealed that since the beginning of time, God has used various forces to form planet Earth as we know it. There are two kinds of forces that we know about. These are constructive forces and destructive forces.

Constructive Forces are forces that tend to build up land areas. Earthquakes and volcanoes are examples of these constructive forces.

Destructive Forces are forces that tend to wear down land areas. The eroding action of running water is an example of this kind of a destructive force.

 Review Exercise IV. A.

1. Who created the planet Earth from nothing? _____

2. What are two constructive forces? _____

3. What is an example of a destructive force? _____

The Creation of the World by Raphael

An earthquake is a sudden shaking or trembling in certain areas of planet Earth. These tremblings are caused by stress deep within the planet. We can learn more about earthquakes by learning first about fault lines, faults, folds, and earthquake belts.

Faults: When the pressure deep within planet Earth is very great, Earth's crust may actually crack or break, and so a huge crack called a fault line, is formed in Earth's crust. One well-known fault line is the San Andreas Fault in California, which can be the cause of future earthquakes.

The great blocks of rock that lie next to one another along a fault line or huge crack are pressed tightly together. Sometimes the two sections of rock on a fault line move suddenly to a new position in order to ease or lessen the pressure from below. The huge blocks of rock may move up and down, sideways, or even pull apart from each other.

Fault Lines

Horst (a block of rock thrown up between normal faults)

Reverse fault

Normal fault

COMPLEX FAULT
Faults very rarely occur singly. Most occur in fault zones along plate margins. The result is often a series of faults, which tilt blocks in many different directions.

The sudden movement of blocks of rock sets up vibrations that shake the Earth many miles away. This shaking is called an earthquake. Some movements may be very small, but others may be very large. Geologists believe that earthquakes were how God caused and formed the great mountain ranges, such as the Sierra Nevada Mountains. These mountains are called fault mountains by the scientists.

Folds: The great temperatures and pressures deep within planet Earth sometimes cause tremendous sideways forces in Earth's crust which make the layers of rock appear to bend and wrinkle. This pushes them into a shape like an ocean wave which is called a fold. Some folds may be very small, but others may be very large. Geologists believe that this is how God caused and formed the great mountain ranges like the Rockies or the Andes. These mountains are called fold mountains.

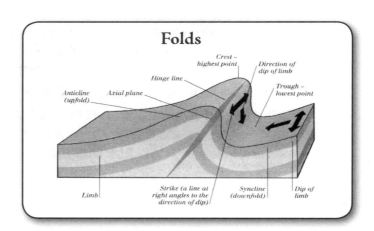

Folds

Crest – highest point
Direction of dip of limb
Hinge line
Anticline (upfold)
Axial plane
Trough – lowest point
Limb
Strike (a line at right angles to the direction of dip)
Syncline (downfold)
Dip of limb

Earthquake belts: Although earthquakes may take place all over planet Earth, earthquakes happen most often along fault lines in two large areas of the Earth. These two areas are called earthquake belts. One earthquake belt circles the Pacific Ocean, and the other is next to the Mediterranean Sea and goes through Central Europe.

Many great saints throughout the history of the Church have said that it is the angels who guide the workings of the natural world on Earth. Some saints believe that these angelic spirits move things on Earth in accordance with the laws that God has laid down for planet Earth, and which scientists then discover. We should never live in fear of the great forces of nature like earthquakes or volcanoes. God controls them all.

We should pray for God's special mercy and protection from destructive forces. The Church knows that God can draw good results even from such events. The Church encourages us to pray for divine protection, both through prayer to God Himself or through the intercession of His angels and saints.

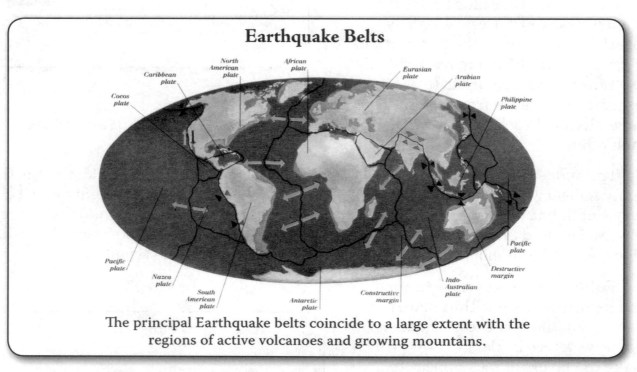

Earthquake Belts

The principal Earthquake belts coincide to a large extent with the regions of active volcanoes and growing mountains.

O God, who has established the Earth upon its firm foundations, graciously hear our prayers in time of disaster. After you have removed the danger, use it as a means of salvation to mankind. Let it remind us of our eternal destiny. We ask this through Christ Our Lord. Amen.

Practical Application: Explore the detection of earthquakes.

Materials: pencil, ruler, compass, map below

To detect an earthquake, scientists use special instruments with which they can pinpoint the origin of the earthquake. These instruments are placed on three points of activity labeled A, B, and C. By examining their instruments, scientists are able to find out how far from the instruments the earthquake occurred.

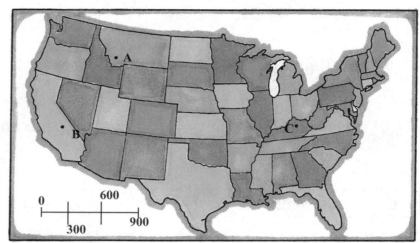

Because of small errors in measurement, the three circles that you will draw with a compass will probably not meet at exactly the same point. They will form a triangle enclosing the epicenter.

For this Practical Application, the scientists have found that an earthquake occurred 900 miles from point A, 1200 miles from point B, and 900 miles from point C.

Step 1: Using the map scale, find out how many inches on the map equal 900 miles. Using the ruler, make a dot on the map that is 900 miles from point A.

Step 2: Put the point of the compass on Point A and set the pencil on the point you marked. Draw a circle around Point A. All points on the circle are 900 miles from Point A. The center of the earthquake will be some point on this circle.

Step 3: Repeat the procedure for Point B. Use the distance of 1200 miles. The center of the earthquake is on the points where the two circles cross.

Step 4: Repeat for Point C, using a distance of 900 miles. The point where the three circles cross is the center of the earthquake.

 Review Exercise IV. B.

1. The great temperatures and pressures within Earth sometimes seem to cause bends and wrinkles in the crust called a _____.

2. The Rockies are called _____ mountains.

3. When the Earth's crust actually cracks or breaks, a _____ is formed.

4. The sudden movement of the great blocks of rock that lie next to one another along a fault line cause an _____.

5. Geologists believe that earthquakes caused great _____ ranges.

6. Earthquakes happen most often in two large areas of the world called _____.

7. One belt circles the _____ Ocean and the other is next to the Mediterranean Sea.

C. Volcanoes

A volcano is like a mountain or hill formed around a crack in planet Earth's crust. The stress deep within the planet sometimes causes a volcano to erupt. This means that hot molten rock, gases, and other hot materials are suddenly thrust and thrown out of the crack.

When the hot molten rock is still below the surface, it is called magma. The opening at the top of a volcano is called a crater. A crater is shaped like a bowl, a depression in the volcano. Sometimes the crater becomes filled with water and forms a lake. When the hot magma breaks through or erupts and flows out of the volcano, then it is called lava. When people look up and see hot liquid rock come down the side of a volcano, they are running from the volcano's lava.

Lava can flow out of the crater at the top of the volcano, like water flowing down the side of the volcano until it cools. Sometimes the lava is sprayed out of the top of the volcano in small droplets to form volcanic dust, which then spreads out far and wide into the atmosphere. However, sometimes the lava is sprayed out as volcanic ash, which falls close to the mountain since it is much heavier than dust particles.

Sometimes the molten rock and other hot materials are not able to break through Earth's surface crust. Then the molten rock can cause the surface to rise like a huge blister. If the blister is huge enough, it can form a mountain called a dome mountain. Geologists believe that this is how the Black Hills of South Dakota were formed. Geologists believe that the Cascade Mountains of Washington state and Oregon were formed because of volcanic eruptions. These are known as dome mountains.

Some volcanoes erupt quietly, like those in Iceland and the Hawaiian Islands. Others, like those in the Mediterranean Sea, erupt violently because of the tremendously huge pressure within them. Some volcanoes alternate between being quiet and being explosive.

There are three main types of volcanoes: **active**, **dormant**, and **extinct**.

An **active** volcano is one which still erupts or has recently erupted.

A **dormant** volcano is one which has not erupted for some time but still shows some signs of activity, such as emitting steam or ash.

An **extinct** volcano is one which has not erupted for some time and shows no sign of activity. However, these sometimes turn into active volcanoes as with Mount St. Helens in Washington state, which erupted on May 18, 1980. This volcano had been extinct for over 123 years.

Eruption of Mt. St. Helens

Some home schooling students have been able to collect volcanic ash from the eruption at Mount St. Helens as part of a science field trip to that area.

Almost all of the volcanoes on Earth are found in the same place as the two earthquake belts. Most of the islands in the Pacific Ocean are actually the tops of extinct volcanoes!

 Practical Application: Investigate the eruption of a volcano.

Materials: clear plastic box, modeling clay, red food coloring, white vinegar, baking soda

Step 1: Use modeling clay to make a model of a volcano that is sliced in half, inside the clear plastic box. Its flat side should be against one side of the box.

Step 2: Remove the volcano model from the box. Use a round pen to make grooves in the flat side of the volcano.

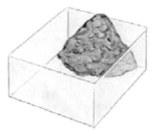

Figure 1

Step 3: Press some baking soda into the grooves, so that it sticks to the clay.

Step 4: Put the model back in the box, with the flat side and the grooves against the side of the box.

Step 5: Put a few drops of red food coloring with the vinegar. Stir the mixture until it is well mixed.

Step 6: Slowly pour the colored vinegar into the opening at the top of the model.

Figure 2

You will observe:

— A liquid bubbles out of the grooves, just like the liquid rock and ash that flow out of openings in volcanoes during an eruption.

— The outside of the model becomes coated with colored liquid, just like the outside of a volcano becomes coated with lava and ash.

— A foam remains inside the volcano, just like magma that remains inside the volcano after an eruption ends.

Review Exercise IV. C.

1. A volcano is like a mountain or hill formed around a _____ in Earth's crust.

2. The stress deep within the planet sometimes causes a volcano to _____.

3. When a volcano erupts, hot materials, gases, and molten _____ are suddenly thrown out of the crack.

4. What is the opening at the top of a volcano called? _____

5. What do we call hot molten rock still below the surface of Earth's crust? _____

6. Many mountain ranges were formed because of _____ activity.

7. A volcano that still erupts or has recently erupted, is known as a _____ volcano.

8. A volcano that still shows some signs of activity is known as a _____ volcano.

9. An extinct volcano can be described as one that shows no signs of activity, but sometimes turns into an _____ volcano.

10. An example of an extinct volcano is _____.

11. Most of the islands in the Pacific Ocean are the tops of _____ volcanoes.

12. What do we call hot molten rock once it starts running down the side of a volcano? _____

Review for Chapter Two

The Moon, Space, and Earth

True or False - Please mark "T" for true or "F" for false

_____ 1. There are clouds on the Moon.

_____ 2. John Glenn was the first American to orbit the earth.

_____ 3. Planet Earth is made up of a number of layers, like an onion.

_____ 4. The layer of soil on top of Earth's crust is very thick.

_____ 5. Earthquakes happen most often in two large areas of the earth.

Please match the words below with their correct definition.

_____ 6. Lunar Eclipse   a. Outer layer of earth

_____ 7. Geology   b. A mountain formed around a crack in Earth's crust through which molten rock is thrown out

_____ 8. Petrology   c. When Earth passes between the Sun and the Moon

_____ 9. Volcano   d. The science that studies rocks

_____ 10. Crust   e. The science that studies the structure of Earth

Please complete the sentences below.

11. Blessed _____ _____ is the founder of the science of Geology.

12. The pull of the Moon's gravity is too weak to hold any _____.

13. During each month the Moon passes through all its phases, going from completely dark to completely _____ and then back to completely dark again.

14. The first person to orbit the earth was _____ _____.

15. By looking at the way _____ travel through planet Earth, geologists believe Earth is made of separate layers.

Please circle the letter of the correct answer.

16. The first men to land on the Moon were:

   a) Blessed Niels Stenson and Nicolaus Copernicus

   b) Neil Armstrong and Edwin Aldrin

   c) John Glenn and Edward White

   d) Yuri Gagarin and Valentina Tereshkova.

17. In a lunar month the Moon goes through the phases of:

   a) Full Moon, Last Quarter, Quarter Moon, New Moon

   b) Quarter Moon, Last Quarter, Full Moon, New Moon

   c) Last Moon, New Moon, Last Quarter, Full Moon

   d) New Moon, First Quarter, Full Moon, Last Quarter

18. Astronomers put their telescopes on high mountains because:

   a) they do not want to be disturbed

   b) they want to be close to the heavens

   c) they want the air to be clear and still

   d) they want to save money

19. The Rockies are an example of:

   a) fold mountains   b) fault mountains

   c) dome mountains   d) volcanoes

20. A force that God has used to wear down land areas is known as:

   a) volcano   b) earthquake   c) gravity   d) running water

God said: "Let the waters that are under the heaven be gathered together into one place: and let the dry land appear." And it was done. And God called the dry land, Earth; and the gathering together of the waters He called Seas.

Gen. 1: 9–10

Introduction

In addition to the Sun, Earth, and the air that we breathe, God gave us the gift of the great oceans. The oceans, filled with salt water, are a major feature of the world. The oceans affect the weather in many ways, especially in regard to rain and the winds. With the abundant fish and other marine and plant life in the oceans, God has provided us with nutritious food.

Blaise Pascal, a Special Scientist

Blaise Pascal was born in 1623 in France. Blaise was the son of Etienne Pascal, a mathematician employed as a tax collector in Rouen. In 1631, after the death of his wife, Etienne moved with his children to Paris. Since they all showed extraordinary intellectual ability, he decided to educate his own children.

Blaise was a child prodigy who showed an amazing aptitude for mathematics and science. At the age of eleven, he composed a treatise on the sounds of vibrating bodies. In 1642, while still a teenager, Blaise started some pioneering work on calculating machines, and eventually invented the mechanical calculator to help his father in his tax collecting work.

Blaise Pascal's influence on mathematics was great. He invented Pascal's triangle, contributed to the philosophy of mathematics and probability theory, invented the hydraulic press, and investigated the properties of air and liquids, among many other subjects.

God gave Blaise Pascal many gifts, which he used to help others. In 1654, Pascal had a religious vision which he recorded, after which he quoted Psalm 119:16: "I will not forget Thy word. Amen." After this, he began writing his first major literary work on religion, the Provincial Letters. He defended the Catholic Faith by word and example. He is also famous for his collection of notes on religion entitled "Pensees" (Thoughts). They have influenced many people to become followers of Jesus.

Blaise Pascal

Pascal was a great Catholic scientist, inventor, writer, and mathematician. He lived about the time that St. Margaret Mary Alacoque, who also lived in France, was receiving visions from Jesus regarding the message of God's infinite love and mercy from the Sacred Heart of Jesus. In 1662, Pascal became ill, received Extreme Unction, and died the next morning, his last words being "May God never abandon me."

 Review Exercise

1. Blaise Pascal was a great scientist, writer, inventor, and _____.

2. As a scientist, Pascal investigated the properties of _____ and liquids.

3. Pascal lived during the 1600s in the country of _____.

4. In addition to the Sun, the most important gift God gave to Earth is the gift of the great _____.

5. The oceans affect the climate in regard to rain and _____.

6. The oceans provide abundant _____ and other marine life.

7. Pascal influenced many people to become _____ of Jesus.

St. Margaret Mary Alacoque Contemplating the Sacred Heart of Jesus

Outline of Chapter Three

I. The Ocean
  - A. The Oceans of Earth
  - B. What the Ocean Does

II. Earth's Atmosphere
  - A. Composition of the Atmosphere
  - B. Purpose of the Atmosphere

III. The Weather
  - A. Influence of Weather
  - B. Causes of Our Weather

IV. Wind and Water in the Atmosphere
  - A. Causes of Winds
  - B. Water in the Atmosphere
    1. Dew and Frost
    2. Rain and Snow
    3. Clouds
  - C. The Water Cycle

Chapter Aims

1. to know the oceans of the world
2. to learn about Earth's atmosphere and why it is so helpful
3. to learn about the weather and what causes it
4. to study the wind and how it helps us
5. to appreciate the gift of water and the water cycle
6. to learn about clouds and what they do for us

Activities

1. study the cause of deep ocean currents
2. see the effects of the atmosphere
3. see why the sky is blue
4. keep a weather chart
5. learn about the Beaufort Wind Scale
6. explore why it rains
7. make a water cycle
8. see why clouds form

I. The Ocean

The ocean is the entire body of salt water that covers more than 70% of planet Earth's surface! The study of the science of the oceans is called oceanography. Scientists who study the ocean are called oceanographers.

A. The Oceans of Earth

Many geographers divide the great waters of Earth into five oceans: the Pacific, the Atlantic, the Indian, the Arctic, and the Southern Ocean. In the year 2000, some oceanographers decided to add the Southern Ocean to the list of oceans because it is so large across the southern part of planet Earth. Oceans cover almost three quarters of the surface of our planet.

The largest and deepest ocean on the planet is the Pacific Ocean. It is bordered by the west coast of North and South America and the east coast continents of Australia and Asia. The states of Alaska, Hawaii, California, Oregon, and Washington have beaches on the Pacific Ocean.

The Atlantic is the second largest and second deepest ocean of planet Earth. It is about two-thirds the size of the Pacific Ocean and is a little less deep. It is bordered by the east coast of North and South America and the west coast of the continents of Europe and Africa. Maine, New York, North Carolina, and Florida are just a few of the many states that border the Atlantic Ocean.

The Indian Ocean is the third largest ocean of Earth. It is about one-third the size of the Atlantic Ocean. It is bordered by the east coast of Africa, the southern coast of Asia, and the west coast of Australia.

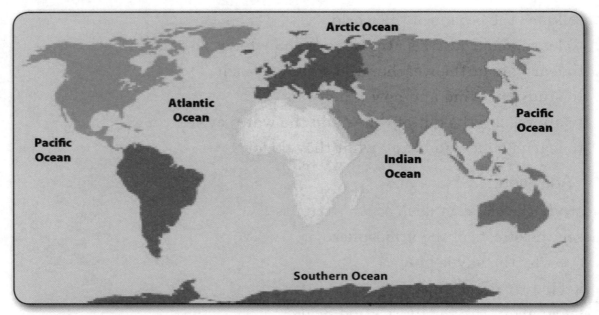

The Southern Ocean is the fourth largest ocean. It is a large body of water totally circling the continent of Antarctica where the South Pole is located. The southern parts of the Atlantic, Pacific, and Indian Oceans are in the southern part of planet Earth.

The Arctic is the fifth largest ocean and is in the northern part of Earth, where the North Pole is located. The Arctic Ocean surrounds the Arctic region at the top of the planet.

 Review Exercise I.A.

1. How many great oceans are on planet Earth? _____

2. List the great oceans of Earth, from the largest to the smallest.

    _____

    _____

3. What do we call scientists who study the oceans? _____

4. Where is the Arctic Ocean located? _____

5. Read Matthew 8:24–27 to learn what command Jesus gave the sea.

 Practical Application: Study Deep Ocean Currents.

Materials: a large container, crushed ice, a paper cup, tape, and food coloring

Step 1: Fill the large container with water and leave for a day in order that the temperature throughout the container equalizes.

Step 2: Punch a number of small holes in the bottom of the paper cup.

Step 3: Place the crushed ice in the paper cup and then put a few drops of food coloring in with the ice.

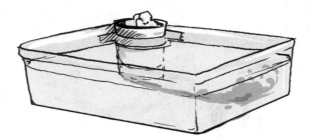

Investigating deep sea currents with a container of water, crushed ice, and a paper clip

Step 4: Lower the cup of crushed ice into the water at one corner of the container and hold it in place by means of tape.

Result: A deep sea current will begin to flow due to the slow movement of cold water from the paper cup to the other side of the container. You will see the current by observing the flow of food coloring. If you place small bits of paper on top of the water, you will see them move towards the paper cup as the water "piles up" at the end of the container.

B. What the Ocean Does

Why did God give us great big oceans?

One reason is that Earth's oceans help reduce any extremes of heat and cold on Earth. The oceans slow down the rate of the changes in temperature between day and night, and summer and winter. The ocean's waters heat up and cool down at a much slower rate than does the land heat up and cool down. Were it not for the oceans, Earth's land surface would suffer great extremes in temperature. It would be much colder at night and much hotter during the day without the warmer ocean waters in the winter and the cooler ocean waters in the summer.

A second reason that God gave us the great big oceans is that Earth's oceans are a great source of food for all the people and animals on Earth. Birds, animals, and human beings eat many of the fish and plants that live in Earth's oceans. Many children like fish sticks and tuna fish!

A third reason that God gave us the great big oceans is that they provide rain water, which is necessary to provide food on dry land. Without the oceans, there would be no rain to fall on dry soil. The atmosphere, from which we get falling rain, obtains most of its water vapor from the oceans! The Sun's rays change seawater into salt-free water vapor in the atmosphere. Much of this water vapor eventually cools, condenses, and falls as rain on some other part of the ocean or land.

Review Exercise I. B.

1. Earth's oceans reduce extremes of heat and _____ upon Earth.

2. The oceans slow down the rate of change in _____ between day and night.

3. Earth's oceans are a great source of _____ for people and animals.

4. Birds, animals, and people eat many of the fish and _____ that live in the ocean.

5. Without the oceans, there would be no _____ to fall upon the soil.

6. Energy from the Sun changes seawater into water _____.

7. Water vapor goes up into the _____.

8. Eventually, the seawater condenses and falls as _____.

A view of the Pacific Ocean

II. Earth's Atmosphere

There is a layer of air around planet Earth which is called the **atmosphere**. The atmosphere extends about 100 miles out from the surface of Earth. The science of the study of the atmosphere is called **meteorology**. Scientists who study the atmosphere of Earth are called **meteorologists**. However, we often call these scientists "weathermen."

A. Composition of the Atmosphere

Meteorologists have found that Earth's atmosphere is mostly a mixture of two gases: nitrogen and oxygen. There are also small quantities of other gases such as carbon dioxide. The oxygen in Earth's atmosphere is the gas that living things on Earth need to breathe in order to live. Oxygen also makes it possible for fire to burn, which is essential to keep people warm by burning fuels.

The atmosphere is essential for life on planet Earth. It is planet Earth's pull of gravity that holds the atmosphere in place around our planet. God gave us the atmosphere as a special protective umbrella and yet as an umbrella that catches water vapor and sends it back down as rain.

Earth's moon has no atmosphere because its pull of gravity is too weak. Space probes have found that other planets have atmospheres. However, the atmosphere of Venus and Mars are mostly carbon dioxide. Carbon dioxide is the gas that we human beings *exhale*. In addition, the atmosphere of Venus is too hot and dense. The atmosphere of Mars is too thin for life. For that reason, human beings cannot live on those planets.

It is Earth's atmosphere that makes the sky appear blue! Earth, upon which Jesus was born, lived, and died, is cloaked in an atmosphere resembling an umbrella in the white and blue colors of the Mother of God. **Astronauts** in space have seen Earth adorned with the blue color of its oceans and the white of its clouds in the atmosphere. So whenever we look at the blue sky, we are reminded that Mary always has her mantle of blue and white around her children on Earth.

Practical Application: See the effects of the atmosphere.

Materials: a 2-liter plastic soda bottle, hot water

Step 1: Carefully fill the soda bottle halfway with hot water.

Step 2: Shake the bottle vigorously.

Step 3: Empty the bottle and quickly screw the cap on tight.

Step 4: Wait and observe the bottle. A gentle inward buckling of the bottle will occur as the atmospheric pressure causes the bottle to collapse, due to the imbalance of pressure on the bottle. When you put the hot water in the bottle, you caused some of the air in the empty bottle to be forced out. When you quickly put the cap on, you prevented the air from being able to re-enter. This difference in pressure caused the bottle to collapse.

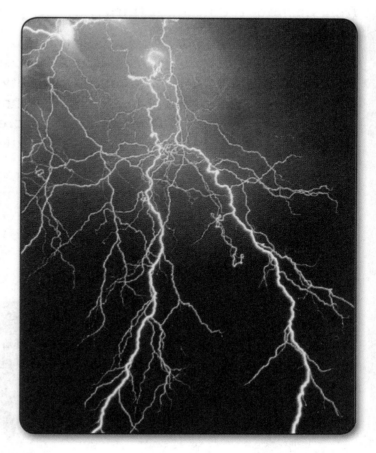

Review Exercise II. A.

1. The science of the study of the atmosphere is called _____.

2. The layer of air around planet Earth is called the _____.

3. The pull of _____ holds Earth's atmosphere in place.

4. What three gases dominate in Earth's atmosphere?

   _____

5. From space, Earth's _____ make the sky appear blue.

6. On Earth, the _____ makes the sky appear blue.

7. _____ is the gas living things need to breathe in order to live.

B. Purpose of the Atmosphere

The atmosphere around Earth serves several purposes. One purpose is to reduce extremes of heat and cold upon Earth. A second purpose is to protect people from harmful radiation. A third purpose is to protect us from meteorites.

Why do you suppose God placed an atmosphere around planet Earth? Earth's atmosphere reduces extremes of heat and cold upon Earth. The atmosphere slows down the changes in temperature between day and night, and slows down the changes in temperature between summer and winter. Were it not for our atmosphere, Earth's surface would suffer great extremes in temperature, just like the Moon's. We would freeze at night and die from the heat during the day.

Earth's umbrella-type atmosphere protects us from the steady stream of meteors that travel toward planet Earth from outer space. Remember that meteors are particles in outer space that frequently strike Earth's atmosphere. Scientists guess that millions of these little particles strike Earth's atmosphere every day. As they fly toward Earth, meteors turn into dust and gas through friction with Earth's atmosphere.

Atmospheric gases scatter blue wavelengths of visible light more than other wavelengths, giving the Earth's visible edge a blue halo.
Image Credit: NASA Earth Observatory

Our atmosphere protects us from harmful radiation from the Sun, too. The upper part of Earth's atmosphere absorbs most of the ultraviolet rays coming from the Sun. Ultraviolet rays can produce sunburn if our skin is exposed to them for too long.

Another part of the atmosphere protects us from the harmful electrically-charged particles that come from the Sun.

Without the atmosphere, there would be no rain to fall on dry soil to produce food, no winds to push hot air away and push cool air close, and no clouds to move in the sky. With no atmosphere, we would have no change from constant sunlight. It is because of the changes that take place within Earth's atmosphere that we experience various types of weather during winter, spring, summer, and fall.

 Practical Application: Learn why the sky is blue.

Materials: flashlight, clear glass of water, a little milk

Step 1: In a dark room, shine the flashlight through the clear glass of water. Look at the beam from the side so you can see the scattered light. Look also at the transmitted light, by reflecting it from a sheet of paper.

Step 2: Now add a little milk, one or two drops at a time and stir the water. The scattered light will become bluish as the transmitted light becomes yellowish and then reddish.

What you are observing is blue light which is scattered more by molecules than is the red light.

Light reaching your eyes from the sky is sunlight that has been scattered by the air molecules and is, therefore, mostly blue. During sunrise or sunset, the light from the Sun must travel at an angle through more of the atmosphere. Red light is able to travel farther through the atmosphere than blue light, so the sky appears a gorgeous orange or red at sunrise and at sunset.

Step 3: As you add more milk, the scattered light becomes white because of repeated scattering and you have made a white cloud.

Sunrise over the Ocean

Review Exercise II. B.

1. Earth's atmosphere reduces any extremes of heat and _____ upon Earth.

2. Earth's atmosphere protects man from the steady stream of _____ particles that strike planet Earth.

3. The atmosphere protects us from harmful _____ rays from the Sun.

4. Harmful rays from the Sun produce_____ when our skin is exposed to them.

5. It is because of the _____that take place within the atmosphere that we experience the various types of weather during the four seasons.

6. Without the atmosphere, there would be no _____ to produce food, and no _____ to fly airplanes.

Cloud front and sunshine

III. The Weather

We think of the weather as the state or condition of the air in the atmosphere at a particular time and place. We think about the temperature, the wind, and the rain or sunshine.

We know that we have four seasons of the year, and that in summer the weather is usually hot, sometimes rainy, while in winter it is very cold, sometimes snowy and icy.

The changes in the air and in Earth's atmosphere that make our weather are caused by the Sun's heat that surrounds Earth. It is the Sun's heat that warms the seas and the land. This heat in the seas and land daily goes back into the air and causes various changes in the atmosphere. So weather can be described as a condition resulting from the atmosphere that changes from time to time depending on temperature, moisture, pressure, and wind.

Having a weather report is important. The weather affects how we live.

Christ Calming the Storm
By Rembrandt

A. Influence of Weather

Weather conditions greatly influence life on Earth and the activities of people. Day to day weather can be hot or cold, wet or dry, calm or stormy, clear or cloudy. Having a weather report is important because the wind, temperature, and rain affect our day-to-day living and working conditions. Farmers plant their crops according to the amount of rain God sends, and how warm or cold it is likely to be. We dress in the morning according to the weather we expect for the day. How we travel depends on the weather, whether we ride our bike or walk or take a bus. We hope for good weather when we plan a picnic or a parade.

Weather is influential in the decisions we make every day, such as deciding when, where, and how to go on our vacation.

In the Byzantine Catholic Liturgy, we pray "For seasonable weather, for an abundance of the fruits of Earth, and for peaceful times."

St. Joseph, the Guardian of the Holy Family
and Patron of Workers, is a powerful intercessor for favorable weather.

"O Heavenly Father, grant through the intercession of St. Joseph, the humble workman whom You chose to watch over Your Son, the grace of favorable weather, so we can do Your Will. We ask this through Christ Our Lord. Amen."

Charting Weather

 Practical Application: Keep a weather chart.

Materials: weather chart, calendar, thermometer, compass, Beaufort scale, weather vane

Step 1: Using the Weather Chart, keep a record of the weather for a month. Keep a record of newspaper forecasts at the same time, and compare them. You will record:

Date: Record the day of the month at the beginning of each line.

Time: Record the time that your observation was made, try to make your observation at the same time every day.

Air Temperature: Measure the outdoor air temperature.

Sky Condition: Determine if the sky is clear, partly cloudy or cloudy.

Rain/Snow: Indicate whether it is raining or snowing.

Wind Speed: Use the Beaufort Wind scale to measure the force of wind over land and sea. Record this.

Wind Direction: Use the points of the compass and a weather vane to record this.

Step 2: Compare the forecasts and the records you have taken. How often do they agree?

Examine the monthly chart you have made. Is there any pattern in the weather?

A tornado observed by a NOAA* team on May 3, 1999, in central Oklahoma
*National Oceanic and Atmospheric Administration

Weather Chart

Date	Time	Outdoor Temp	Clear/Cloudy	Rain or Snow	Wind Speed	Wind Direction

Review Exercise III. A.

1. Weather is the condition of the _____ in the atmosphere in terms of wind, temperature, and rain at a particular time and place.

2. The changes in Earth's atmosphere that are the basis for weather are caused by the Sun's _____ that falls on Earth.

3. The three main ingredients of the weather are the Sun, the wind, and _____ in the atmosphere.

B. Causes of Our Weather

The weather outside our homes is due to the temperature and humidity of the atmosphere over the area in which we live. Our weather changes because the winds cause the mass of air over our area to be replaced by a mass of air from some other area. This new mass of air has a different temperature and humidity.

When a meteorologist tries to predict tomorrow's weather, he must look at the way the various masses of air move about Earth's surface and see what particular mass of air will be over the area in which you live. If the new mass of air is cold and has a low humidity, then your area will experience cold temperatures and dry weather. If the new air mass is warm and has a high humidity, then your area will experience warm and rainy weather. Remember that humidity refers to the amount of water vapor in the air.

To help him in his work, a meteorologist uses pictures from weather satellites orbiting Earth. He also uses measurements of wind speed, temperature, and humidity taken at many points over the surface of Earth. As much as he tries, the weatherman is not always right about what the weather will be like. There is always room for surprises.

God is always in control of the weather. He permits bad weather, such as hurricanes or droughts, to remind us of our dependence on Him. But He sends us nice weather as a gift, for which we should thank Him..

Review Exercise III. B.

1. The weather outside your home is due to the _____ and humidity of the atmosphere over the area where you live.

2. Weather changes because the _____ cause the mass of air in one area to be replaced by a mass of air from another area.

3. When a meteorologist tries to predict tomorrow's weather, he must look at the way the various masses of air move about Earth's _____ and see what particular mass of air will be over the area in which you live.

4. Humidity refers to the amount of _____ _____ in the air.

5. Compose a prayer thanking God, our Heavenly Father, for another beautiful day.

An original image of pilgrims
observing the Miracle of the Sun
in Fatima, Portugal on October 13, 1917.

IV. Wind and Water in the Atmosphere

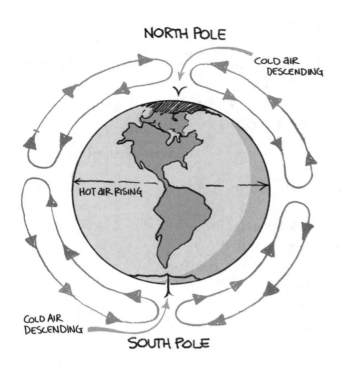

NORTH POLE

COLD AIR DESCENDING

HOT AIR RISING

COLD AIR DESCENDING

SOUTH POLE

How air would circulate over the surface of the Earth if the Earth did not spin on its axis

Wind is the movement of air caused by unequal heating of Earth's surface by the Sun. Earth's surface has different temperatures depending mainly on the location on the planet. The equator is an imaginary line around the center of Earth's globe, at equal distance from the North and South poles. The North Pole is at the very top of planet Earth, and the South Pole is at the very bottom of planet Earth. The hottest places on Earth are close to the Equator, and the coldest places on Earth are close to the poles.

We can compare the movement of air to heating a pot of water on the stove. When we heat a pot of water, the warm water rises from the bottom of the pot, and the cold water above rushes down to take the place of the warm water. In the same way, when the warmer air from Earth's equator rises and pushes north or south toward the poles, the cold air above rushes downward to take the warm air's place.

Wind is essential in moving warm and cold air around the planet to keep temperatures moderate or fairly mild on Earth. People could not live in very very hot or very very cold temperatures. The wind causes weather changes which we need in order to survive on Earth. We must thank God for the wind and the good weather He sends us every day. We think of God when we see the trees and flowers grow and the rivers and oceans flow. We need to think of God also when we feel the winds blow.

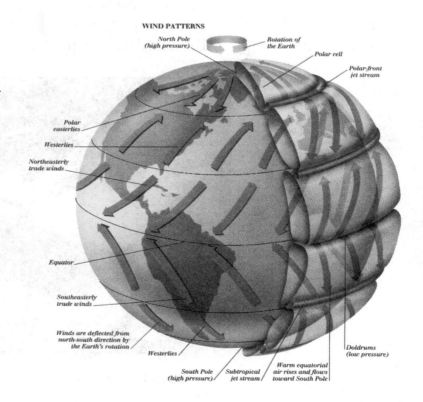

WIND PATTERNS

North Pole (high pressure)

Rotation of the Earth

Polar cell

Polar-front jet stream

Polar easterlies

Westerlies

Northeasterly trade winds

Equator

Southeasterly trade winds

Winds are deflected from north-south direction by the Earth's rotation

Westerlies

Doldrums (low pressure)

South Pole (high pressure)

Subtropical jet stream

Warm equatorial air rises and flows toward South Pole

Practical Application: Learn about the Beaufort Wind Scale.

Wind speeds are most easily measured by using a scale known as the Beaufort Wind Scale. This wind speed scale was invented by Admiral Francis Beaufort over 150 years ago to help people measure the force of wind and speed by observation rather than by taking measurements with instruments.

The Beaufort Wind Scale:

#	Name	Effects	Wind Speed in m.p.h.
0	Calm	Smoke rises vertically	less than 1
1	Light air	Smoke drifts	1 – 3
2	Light breeze	Wind felt on face; leaves rustle Weather vane moved by wind	4 – 7
3	Gentle breeze	Leaves and twigs in constant motion Wind blows small flag	8 – 12
4	Moderate Breezes	Dust and loose paper move Small branches are moved	13 – 18
5	Fresh Breeze	Small leafy trees sway	19 – 24
6	Strong Breeze	Large branches move	25 – 31
7	Moderate Gale	Whole trees in motion	32 – 38
8	Fresh Gale	Twigs broken off trees; hard to walk	39 – 46
9	Strong Gale	Slight damage to buildings	47 – 54
10	Gale	Considerable structural damage Trees uprooted	55 – 63
11	Storm	Widespread damage	64 – 75
12	Hurricane	Excessive damage	over 75

Example of # 12 Hurricane Wind

A. Causes of Winds

The shape of Earth's surface causes it to be heated unequally by the Sun. At the equator, the Sun's rays strike Earth's surface directly, thus concentrating the Sun's energy over a small area. However, away from the equator, the Sun's rays strike Earth's surface at an angle, spreading its energy over a wide area.

At noon, we feel the Sun's heat more because it shines directly down upon us. At any other time of the day, when it shines down upon us at an angle, it doesn't feel as warm. So we know that different areas of Earth's surface are heated unequally at different times.

The differences in heating and cooling between various parts of a continent can cause winds. People often talk about warm mountain breezes rising during the heat of the day, and cool valley breezes coming down a mountain at night.

Another cause of winds is the daily spin of planet Earth. Earth spins around every 24 hours on its axis. The axis is an imaginary line which runs from the North Pole to the South Pole. It represents the angle at which Earth spins; the planet Earth does not spin straight up and down, but spins at an angle. If you purchase a globe on a stand, most likely the Earth will be set at an angle, along its axis line.

Since Earth is spinning on its axis, the moving air is pushed sideways, just as we are pushed sideways on a merry-go-round when we try to walk towards the center. Because of this pushing, a series of wind belts is set up around Earth. The winds in these belts move in a definite direction.

The wind that blows outside our door is affected by the land, mountains, lakes, and oceans around us. Land and water affect the temperature of the wind because land and water have different temperatures, and they do not heat up or cool off at the same rate. Water stores more heat than land, so the oceans and other bodies of water are warmer than the land.

In addition, the oceans warm and cool much slower than land. The Sun is able to warm only the thin upper surface of the land so land is more quickly heated, while the oceans warm and cool much slower than land.

Land breezes and sea breezes are different temperatures also because of the difference in temperature during the day and during the night. Seasonal winds come in the winter because land on the continents is cooler than water in the oceans. In the summer, however, seasonal winds happen because land is warmer than ocean water.

The wind reminds us of the Holy Spirit, the Third Person of the Blessed Trinity. Remember the wind blowing on Pentecost Sunday?

Do you remember when God used the wind to separate the Red Sea so that Moses and the Hebrews could cross it on foot?

Do you remember the miracle Jesus performed when He was in a boat during a storm, and Jesus calmed the wind? The apostles said among themselves, "Who is this that both wind and sea obey Him?" They realized that only God can work miracles that involve nature, such as calming the wind and sea and storms.

Review Exercise IV. A.

1. Wind is the movement of air caused by the unequal _____ of Earth's surface.

2. The _____ is an imaginary line around the center of Earth.

3. The North Pole and the South Pole are close to the two _____ places on Earth.

4. The _____ causes weather changes.

5. At the equator, the Sun's rays strike Earth's surface _____.

6. Away from the equator, the Sun's rays strike Earth's surface at an _____.

7. At _____, the Sun's rays shine down directly on us.

8. Earth's _____ is an imaginary line which runs from the North Pole to the South Pole.

9. Since Earth spins on its axis, the moving air is pushed _____.

10. Because of air being pushed by Earth's spin, a series of _____ are set up around Earth.

11. Land and water affect the _____ of the wind.

12. Oceans are _____ than the land during winter.

B. Water in the Atmosphere

Water vapor is the result of evaporation. Evaporation is a process in which water is turning from a liquid to a gas. When we see a pot of water boil, we see that there is something rising out of the water that we call steam. What we are seeing is water being changed from a liquid to a gas; we say that the water is evaporating. When the water finally becomes a gas, we give it a special name: water vapor.

After a rain shower, we notice evaporation occurring when we see puddles of water on a street. As the Sun starts shining, the puddles slowly start drying up. This water becomes vaporized, turns into water vapor, then rises upwards like a gas, and eventually becomes part of the gases in the atmosphere surrounding Earth.

1. Dew and Frost

Often water vapor changes back into water. This process of change is called **condensation**. Condensation is the opposite of evaporation. Condensation occurs because the temperature of the atmosphere higher up is lower than the temperature of the atmosphere at lower levels.

To understand condensation, let's show an example. When we are in a warm room and a pitcher of ice water is placed on the dining room table, we can see a layer of water slowly forming on the outside of the pitcher of cold water. This is condensation.

In order for the water vapor high up in the atmosphere to condense and form water droplets, the temperature must lower to a certain point. The name given to that low temperature for condensation to occur is called the **dew point**.

Dew is a type of condensation that take place at night on objects near the surface of Earth. We can see dew in the morning on the grass or a parked car. These objects cool very rapidly and the temperature of the air near them is lower than the dew point so that condensation occurs.

If the dew point is **not below** the freezing point of water (0° C), then the water vapor condenses in the form of droplets of water, called **dew**. If the dew point is below the freezing point, the water vapor turns directly into tiny ice crystals called **frost**.

2. Rain and Snow

When water vapor condenses and falls from the atmosphere onto Earth's surface, it does so in the form of rain, sleet, hail, drizzle, or snow.

Rain is the water that falls from a cloud. A cloud is made of very small droplets of water. When it rains, the little droplets of water join together to form larger drops. These large drops are much heavier than the tiny droplets of water that form the cloud. So the heavy drops fall as rain on Earth. If the rain freezes as it falls through the cold air, we see a type of rain called sleet. Sometimes we see hailstones! Hailstones are lumps of ice, which often pick up dust and dirt as they come down! Watch out!

When the air is very still, then some of the bigger droplets of water that make up a cloud no longer float up in the air. It is the air movement that keeps clouds up. With very little air movement, the droplets slowly fall to the surface of Earth, forming a special type of rain called drizzle. We usually think of drizzle as rain of small drops. We think of drizzle as soft and quiet. Drizzle is nice to have when you have a new garden growing and don't want all your seeds to wash away!

Close up showing crystal structure of Snowflakes

When the temperature of the air is below freezing, the water vapor turns into the form of ice crystals or snow. Because these are so heavy, they fall to the ground. The beautiful six-sided crystals may fall separately if the air near the ground is cold, otherwise they tend to melt together to form wet sticky snow.

A good prayer to say when you see a beautiful snowfall is: *"Wash me, Lord, clean my heart of sin, make it white as snow!"*

 Practical Application: Explore why it rains.

Materials: a kettle, a source of heat, a pan of ice, and a large pan

Step 1: Boil the water. You will see a cloud of water vapor rise in the air from the kettle. We call this water vapor, steam.

Step 2: Place the pan under the vapor.

Step 3: Hold the pan of ice near the cloud of water vapor from the kettle. This makes the cloud cold.

Step 4: When the drops of water are cooled, they come together to form larger drops. These large drops are heavy and begin to fall.

Review Exercise IV. B.

1. When water changes to water vapor, the means by which it does so is called _____.

2. When water becomes like a gas, we call it _____ _____.

3. When water vapor changes back into water, it does so by means of a process called _____.

4. We can see condensation happening in a warm room when we see droplets of _____ forming on the outside of a pitcher of cold water.

5. Dew is a type of condensation that takes place at _____ on objects near the surface of Earth.

6. If the dew point is not below the freezing point of water, then the water vapor turns to _____.

7. Large drops of water are much heavier than the tiny droplets of water that form the clouds, and so they fall as _____ on Earth.

8. When the air is very still, the small drops of water that form the cloud no longer float in the air and slowly fall to Earth as a type of rain called _____.

9. When the temperature of the air is below the freezing point, then the water vapor condenses as _____.

10. If rain freezes as it falls, we see a type of rain called _____.

11. _____ are lumps of ice that often pick up dust and dirt as they fall to Earth.

3. Clouds

A cloud we see up in the sky is a mass of water droplets that is suspended in the atmosphere above the surface of Earth. Clouds are the result of condensation that occurs when a mass of air within the atmosphere is cooled below its dew point. The water vapor usually condenses around tiny particles of dust or salt in the air. The droplets of water in a cloud are so small that slight winds within the atmosphere keep them afloat. Fog is a cloud that is formed on the ground or very near the ground.

The shapes of clouds depend on how they are formed. If the air from which the cloud is formed is moving straight up, then the clouds form in large billowing masses; if the air is moving straight across the sky, then the clouds form in layers.

Types of clouds:

Cirrus: the name cirrus means "curl." These clouds are so named because they tend to look like thin wisps of wool or cotton. They are the highest clouds in the sky, from 4 miles to 8 miles high. They are made up of tiny ice crystals, since the dew point high up in Earth's atmosphere is low.

Cumulus: the name cumulus means "heap." These clouds are so named because they tend to look like large fluffy heaps of wool or cotton. They are usually connected with fair weather. On hot summer days, cumulus clouds may grow very large and dark, causing afternoon thunderstorms.

Stratus: the name stratus means "layer." These clouds are so named because they are made up of layers. They are the clouds nearest Earth. The water vapor in stratus clouds tends to condense in the form of tiny water droplets. Fog is a stratus cloud at the surface of Earth.

Sometimes weathermen like to give a cloud two names. A cloud is given two names because it is like two of the basic types of clouds. So a cirrostratus cloud looks a little like a mixture of cirrus and stratus clouds.

Scientists also attach other words to the basic cloud names in order to describe clouds more accurately: "alto" meaning high; "nimbus" meaning rain; and "fracto" meaning broken. You may have heard a weatherman refer to clouds such as "cumulonimbus" or "altostratus"!

The clouds are helpful to us because they help moderate or keep mild the temperatures on Earth. Have you noticed how cool it gets on a night without any clouds? Without the clouds, the temperatures here on Earth would be much hotter some times and much colder other times.

Dark clouds which carry more water vapor are especially important and useful because they carry rain to different parts of Earth. We pray for rain when we need fruit trees and vegetable plants to grow. Farmers count on the clouds and falling rain to produce the food we all need.

Ascension of Christ
By Garofalo

MAJOR CLOUD TYPES	ALT.	INTERMEDIATE CLOUD TYPES

CIRRUS: Thin, wispy, and feathery. Composed entirely of ice-crystals. Often appear as thin feathery strands known as "mares' tails".

5 mi.

HIGH CLOUDS

CIRROCUMULUS: Thin and patchy. Often form wavelike patterns. Rippled and rare.

CIRROSTRATUS: Thin sheets that look like fine gauze. Gives the sky milky appearance.

3 mi.

MIDDLE CLOUDS

CUMULUS: Puffy, thick, dome-shaped. Cotton-ball appearance. Usually have a flat base.

ALTOCUMULUS: Patches or layers of puffy and rounded appearance. Made of water not ice.

ALTOSTRATUS: Dense veils or sheets that are often lightly striped or streaked.

2 mi.

LOW CLOUDS

STRATOCUMULUS: Irregular puffy masses spread out in a rolling layer.

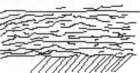

CUMULONIMBUS: Large, thick, thunderstorm clouds. These produce violent weather and tornadoes.

NIMBOSTRATUS: Low and shapeless. Streaked with rain and dark colored.

1 mi.

STRATUS: Low, uniform sheets or layers. Dull to dark gray. Fog if at the ground level.

Practical Application: Observe Clouds

Materials: a 2-liter wide-mouth jar, a box of matches, a rubber glove

Step 1: Put a little water in the 2-liter wide-mouth jar. Cover the jar and allow it to stand for a few hours.

Step 2: Light a match, blow it out, and hold it for a few seconds in the jar. Recover the jar with the rubber glove stretched tightly over the opening.

Step 3: After a few minutes, pull the glove upward sharply. Pulling the rubber cover upwards decreases the pressure inside the jar and produces cooling. The air is cooled to the dew-point temperature. The smoke particles in the jar act as condensation points and make it easier for cloud droplets to form.

If the rubber glove is pushed into the jar, the pressure inside the jar increases and produces heating. The temperature rises above the dew-point and the cloud droplets evaporate.

 Review Exercise IV. C.

1. The tiny droplets of water that form a cloud stay afloat because of the
    _____ in the atmosphere.

2. Fog is a _____ close to the ground.

3. Cirrus type clouds are _____ in the sky and are made up of
    tiny _____ crystals.

4. Cumulus type clouds are connected with _____ weather.

5. Stratus type clouds are clouds _____ to earth and made up of
    many layers.

6. Why is a cloud sometimes given two names? _____

    _____

C. The Water Cycle

Water on Earth is continually evaporating from the oceans, lakes, rivers, soil, and living things to form water vapor. This water vapor is also continually condensing back into water. It returns to Earth as dew or rain. This constant cycle of evaporation and condensation is called the water cycle.

By means of the water cycle, water is continually circulating from oceans, lakes, and rivers to land areas. This gives us the water we need to live. It is wonderful to realize that some of the water that caused the Flood in Noah's time or water that Jesus walked upon may have touched you in some way.

It is also by means of the water cycle that the water of our planet is purified. When water evaporates, all the minerals, mud, and debris that are mixed with it are left behind and so the water that falls back on Earth is relatively pure and clean.

Water is very important in the sacramental life of the Catholic Faith. During the Holy Sacrifice of the Mass, before the Consecration, the priest mixes a little water with the wine in the chalice. The priest also uses water to purify his hands during Mass. Furthermore, water is an essential part of the sacrament of Baptism. As a daily routine, we use holy water as a sacramental when we bless ourselves.

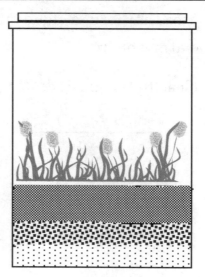

The jar behaves as a miniature Earth, reflecting its water cycle. The water placed in the soil is evaporated by the sunlight. It condenses on the cooler outer surface of the jar and falls like rain on the plants.

Practical Application: See a water cycle.

Materials: a jar with a lid, pebbles, broken charcoal, soil, a few small plants, some water

Step 1: Put a layer of pebbles and then a layer of broken charcoal in the bottom of the jar. Add some soil and moisten it thoroughly.

Step 2: Clean the inside of the jar and place some plants in the soil. One can use any small plant like ferns or evergreen plants.

Step 3: Screw the lid onto the jar. Place the jar in strong (but not direct) sunlight. Let the jar sit and observe what happens.

 Review Exercise IV. D.

1. The constant cycle of evaporation and condensation that happens to water is called the _____ _____.

2. By means of the water cycle, water is continually moved from oceans, lakes, and rivers to _____ areas.

3. It is also by means of the water cycle that water is cleaned and _____.

4. When water _____, all the minerals and mud are left behind.

5. Water is an essential part of the sacrament of _____.

Review for Chapter Three

The Oceans, the Weather, and the Climate

True or False - Please mark "T" for true or "F" for false.

_____ 1. The oceans cover almost three quarters of Earth's surface.

_____ 2. Oceans cause great extremes of temperature on Earth.

_____ 3. The weather outside our homes is due to the temperature and humidity where we live.

_____ 4. Wind is caused by the rotation of Earth.

_____ 5. Rain is water that falls from a cloud.

Please match the numbered words with the letters of its correct definitions.

_____ 6. Blaise Pascal

_____ 7. Meteorology

_____ 8. Admiral Beaufort

_____ 9. Water cycle

_____ 10. Oceanography

a. Invented a scale to measure wind speed

b. The science that studies the oceans

c. Constant cycle of evaporation and condensation

d. The science that studies the atmosphere

e. Investigated the properties of air and liquids

Please complete the sentences.

11. There are _____ great oceans of the world.

12. The Moon has no atmosphere because its pull of _____ is so weak.

13. Weather reports help farmers know when to _____ their crops.

14. _____ is the movement of air caused by the unequal heating of Earth's surface by the Sun.

15. Water vapor in the atmosphere condenses back to water when the atmospheric temperature falls below the _____ _____.

Please circle the letter of the correct answer.

16. Earth's oceans do not:

    a) moderate the temperatures on earth   b) provide food for living creatures

    c) protect us from meteorites   d) provide rain

17. Without the atmosphere, there would be no:

    a) weather   b) protection from radiation

    c) life on earth   d) all of these

18. The weather is caused by:

    a) the Sun's heat that falls on Earth   b) the water in the atmosphere.

    c) the wind   d) all of these

19. The amount of water vapor in the atmosphere depends on:

    a) the pull of gravity   b) the wind

    c) the temperature   d) the presence of clouds

20. What is not a type of cloud:

    a) solar   b) cumulus   c) stratus   d) cirrus

"Whosoever drinketh of this water, shall thirst again;
but he that shall drink of the water that I will give him, shall not thirst forever."

John 4:13

Introduction

Marie Sklodowska Curie was a famous scientist who was born in Catholic Poland. She spent many years of her life studying matter. In 1867, she moved to France to study at the Sorbonne University. There she met and married Pierre Curie who was also a scientist. Together they worked on many experiments in physics and chemistry. They studied the newly discovered phenomenon of radioactivity, which dealt with the breakup of one kind of matter into another kind of matter.

In 1898, the Curies announced the discovery of a new element which they named Polonium, after the country of Marie's origin, Poland. For their work on radioactivity, the Curies were together awarded the Nobel Prize in Physics in 1903. Marie was the first woman to ever receive this prize.

The discoveries of the Curies were important because they helped scientists to study and to learn about God's laws for material things, also called matter, found in our world.

In 1911, Madame Curie, as she was called in France, received a second award, this time the Nobel Prize in Chemistry, for discovering radium. Radium sends out powerful rays which destroy cancer cells. We call this process radiation.

Marie Curie

Madame Curie was a humanitarian who wished to use her knowledge and research for the good of mankind and the glory of God. Because of her work, X-rays are very common today. X-rays today provide a non-invasive way (nonsurgical) to examine the internal organs of the body.

Madame Curie died in France in 1934. She lived during the time that the Blessed Mother appeared at Fatima, and the time during which St. Therese of Lisieux lived in France.

It is likely that Madame Curie was familiar with the Fatima apparition. It is possible that she prayed for heavenly aid as she worked on her research. Certainly those whose lives are changed because of life-saving radiation owe a great debt to God and to Marie Curie for helping to save lives through radiation.

1. Marie Curie was a French scientist who discovered the elements polonium and _____ .

2. For discovering these elements, Madame Curie was awarded the _____ _____ in Chemistry.

3. _____ is the process during which radium sends out powerful rays.

4. Madame Curie's discoveries were important in helping scientists study God's laws for _____ things, or matter.

5. Radium sends out powerful rays that destroy _____ cells.

6. X-rays provide a non-invasive or non-surgical way to examine the _____ organs of the human body.

A cyclotron produces a beam that is used to treat certain forms of cancer.

Outline

I. Matter: Material Things
   A. Basic Properties of Matter
   B. Three Forms of Matter
II. Solids
   A. Solid Matter
   B. Solids and Temperature
   C. Solids and Liquids
III. Liquids
   A. Liquid Matter
   B. Liquids and Temperature
   C. Solids, Liquids, and Gases
   D. The Uniqueness of Water
IV. Gases
   A. Gaseous Matter
   B. Gases and Temperature
   C. Gases and Liquids

Basilica at Lisieux

Chapter Aims

1. know the properties of matter
2. know the three forms of matter and their differences
3. know what is the difference between temperature and heat
4. know how solids, liquids, and gases behave when heated

Activities:

1. learn how we measure temperature
2. study how heat changes solids to liquids
3. see how a metal expands when heated
4. see that the freezing points of materials are different
5. see the effects of the thermal expansion of water
6. study the strange behavior of water's volume
7. show that air has weight
8. see that a gas expands when heated

I. Matter: Material Things

Scientists call material things "matter." The world is full of matter or material things that we can experience through our senses. It is the physical properties of matter which we experience through our sense of sight, smell, hearing, taste, and touch. Material objects, such as wood, air, water, plants, soil, and all other matter have definite properties which allow us to see the differences among them. We study the properties of matter in order to learn how different things are made, and how things react to different processes found in nature.

A. Basic Properties of Matter

1. All matter has weight.

If you lift a book, it feels heavy. It wants to move towards the floor. This heaviness is what we call weight. The book wants to move towards the floor because Earth's gravity pulls all objects near it towards the center of the earth. Weight is the gravitational attraction, or pull, between two bodies. The larger the two bodies are, and the closer together they are, the stronger the attraction between them.

2. All matter has mass.

The mass of an object is related to its reluctance to being pushed. It is easier to push a shopping cart than a car. This is because the shopping cart has less mass than the car. The amount of matter in an object is called its mass.

On Earth, we think of mass and weight as the same thing. However, the mass of an object always stays the same. But, since the weight of an object depends on Earth's pull of gravity, the weight can change.

Remember that the pull of gravity on the Moon is much less than on Earth. Gravity is less on the Moon because the mass of the Moon, is much much less than the mass of the Earth; consequently, there is not as much "pull" of gravity on the Moon. If we were to go to the Moon, we would weigh much less, although our size or mass would be the same as on Earth. When we see pictures of the astronauts floating in the space ships, that is because their ships have flown way beyond planet Earth's pull of gravity. Basically, the Earth's gravity keeps our feet on the ground!

3. All matter has volume.

Matter takes up space, so matter has volume. Volume means that the matter or material thing has length, width, and height. These three properties are called the dimensions of matter. Another common name for volume is size.

The science that deals with what the things around us are made of and the ways they change is called chemistry. The scientists who study chemistry are called chemists. You will learn a little about chemistry in this chapter.

God is not made of matter. He is pure Spirit. So God does not have the properties of matter. Material things occupy a certain space, but God is present everywhere.

 Review Exercise I. A.

1. The _____ of an object is what we call weight.

2. Earth's _____ gives matter the property of weight.

3. The _____ of an object is related to its reluctance to being pushed.

4. Satellites in orbit have equal mass but less _____ than on Earth.

5. Another name for volume is _____.

6. Length, width, and height are called the _____ of matter.

7. God is pure _____.

B. Three Forms of Matter: Solid, Liquid, Gas

Matter on Earth is mainly found in one of three forms. It is either a solid, a liquid, or a gas. All matter can be changed from one form to another form by heating it or by cooling it. Whether a thing is found as a solid, liquid, or gas depends upon its degree of hotness or temperature. The temperature of a material thing is commonly measured in degrees Centigrade. We write °C after the number to denote temperature in degrees Centigrade.

Water is the most common liquid substance found on Earth. It can be found in three forms.

If the temperature of water is below 0° C , then water is found as a solid. Ice is the name given to this solid. An ice cube holds its own shape. It has a definite volume, shape, and size, and takes up a certain amount of space.

The Three Forms of Water

Water Vapor   Water   Ice

If the temperature of water is between 0° C and 100° C, then water is found as a liquid. Water can be formed from solid ice by heating the ice. By cooling water below 0° C, we can make solid ice from the water.

Water is called a liquid because it has a definite volume but no definite shape. This means when you pour water or any liquid into a glass, it stays there, occupying a definite space as it is confined in the glass. However, the water inside the glass has no definite shape. The shape of the mass of water depends on the shape of the glass.

If the temperature of water goes above 100° C, then water is found as a gas. Water vapor, or steam, is the name given to this gas. Water vapor can be formed from water when water is heated above 100° C (that is, when it is boiled).

Water can be formed from water vapor when water vapor is cooled to below 100° C. Water vapor is called a gas because it has neither a definite volume nor a definite shape. This means that when we have water vapor in a container like a pot on the stove, the gas fills the whole space of the pot. Remember the water vapor has no definite shape. The shape of the mass of water vapor depends on the shape of the pot or container, which the gas fills completely.

Practical Application: See how we measure temperature.

Materials: medicine bottle, cork, clear plastic straw or medicine bottle tube, vegetable dye, a pen

Step 1: Fit a medicine bottle or small glass jar with a cork and tube.

Step 2: Fill the bottle to the brim with water colored with a few drops of vegetable dye.

Step 3: Mark the line the water rises to in the tube.

Step 4: Place your bottle in a pot of warm water. Mark the line to which the water rises.

Step 5: Cool the bottle in the refrigerator. Mark the line to where the water falls.

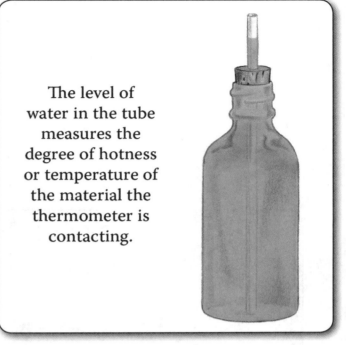

The level of water in the tube measures the degree of hotness or temperature of the material the thermometer is contacting.

You have made a simple thermometer. The marks on the tube tell you the temperature of the thermometer and any objects that are touching it. A Centigrade thermometer shows the mark for the freezing point of water as the number 0 and shows the mark for the boiling point of water as the number 100. Finally, it divides the space between marks on the tube for the freezing point of water and the boiling point of water into 100 steps.

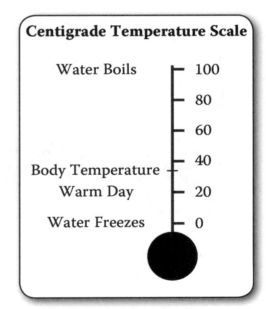

Centigrade Temperature Scale

Water Boils — 100

— 80

— 60

Body Temperature — 40

Warm Day — 20

Water Freezes — 0

 Review Exercise I. B.

1. Everything on planet Earth is found either as a solid, a liquid, or a _____.

2. A thing can be changed from one form to another by _____ or cooling it.

3. If the temperature of water is below 0 ˚C, then water is found as a _____ or ice.

4. If the temperature of water is between 0°C and 100 °C, then water is found as a _____.

5. If the temperature of water is above 100°C, then water is found as a _____, which is called water vapor.

An Image of a Glacier

II. Solids

A solid is a compact, hard, three-dimensional substance. It contrasts with a liquid substance which flows freely. A solid does not flow. Children like throwing solid snowballs, but they would rather be hit by liquid water flowing from a hose on a hot day!

A. Solid Matter

Solid matter has two characteristics.

1. Solid matter has a definite shape.

When you place a cube of sugar on the table top or in an empty glass, it remains a cube of sugar. It holds its familiar cube shape and doesn't spread out like a drop of water does.

2. Solid matter has a definite volume.

The cube of sugar on the table top stays together in one place occupying a certain amount of space. It doesn't spread throughout the room like scent from an open bottle of perfume.

 Review Exercise II. A.

1. Solid matter has a definite _____.

2. Having a definite _____ is another property of a solid.

B. Solids and Temperature

When we increase the temperature of a solid by heating it, we find that its length, width, and height increase; the solid gets larger. This is called thermal expansion. Thermal means heat; the expansion is due to heat.

The amount of expansion a solid undergoes depends on the type of solid. Solids like copper and brass tend to expand a great deal. Materials like plastic and glass expand very little. This is why we can unscrew a hot metal lid from a glass jar. When you heat a metal lid on a sealed glass jar, you can easily unscrew the hot metal lid. The metal lid expands more than the glass and so the heated metal lid is less tightly held than the cool metal lid. Next time you have a jar with a metal lid that you cannot open, try the experiment below.

Engineers must allow for the expansion of solids in everything they build. Look at the concrete pavement upon which we walk. Notice that it is made in sections about 4 feet long. The sections have a small gap between them, which is filled with a very soft material. This allows for the expansion of the concrete sections. If the gaps were not present, then, with changes in temperature [from snow in the winter and hot sunshine in the summer], the sections would push one another upward as they expand. The pavement might crack or become very uneven.

Practical Application: See how a metal expands when heated.

Materials: glass jar with a tight metal lid, hot water from faucet, a towel, kitchen mittens

Step 1: Ask someone stronger than you to screw the lid of the jar on so tightly that you cannot unscrew it.

Step 2: Turn on the hot water faucet. Adjust the water flow to a steady strong stream.

Step 3: Place the jar under the hot water so the hot water falls on the jar lid and down the drain. Let the water run for one or two minutes.

Step 4: Turn off the water. Dry the jar with the towel. With the kitchen mittens on, try to unscrew the lid. Are you surprised how easy it is to unscrew?

Caution: The metal lid will be hot, but do not let it cool before you unscrew it or it will contract back to its original size.

 Review Exercise II. B.

1. When we increase the temperature of a solid by heating it, we find that its length, width, and height _____.

2. This process is called _____ _____.

The Cathedral of Notre Dame in Montreal
What kind of expansion problems might engineers have had in building this cathedral?

C. Solids and Liquids

A solid is a substance that does not flow but is compact and hard. A liquid is a substance that flows freely like water.

If we keep heating a solid, it suddenly stops expanding and slowly changes to a liquid. This change of form is called melting and the temperature at which this occurs is called the melting point.

The change of matter from solid to liquid requires energy. As a solid (like a stick of butter) is melted, heat is absorbed by the solid. The temperature of the butter does not change as much as you would expect because the heat is being used to convert the solid into a liquid. It is only after the butter has all melted that the temperature begins to increase again.

 Practical Application: Study how heat changes solids to liquids.

Parental supervision required!

Materials: pot or tin can, 7 ice cubes, cup of water, electric stove, thermometer (you can use the one you made previously)

Step 1: Place the ice cubes in the pot along with the cup of water.

Step 2: Place the thermometer in the pot, so that you can read the temperature mark. Wait for ten minutes until the level of the liquid in the thermometer has remained constant.

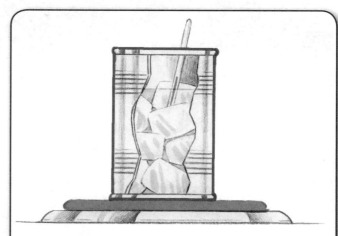

Slowly apply heat to the ice/water mixture and notice how the temperature changes.

Step 3: Slowly apply heat to the ice/water mixture in the pot by placing it on a stove. Do not boil. Turn off the heat within 1 to 2 minutes after the ice melts.

In this experiment, we found that the solid water (ice) melted into liquid water as it was heated. The actual temperature of the melting point varies with the particular material. It can be very low like that of ice which melts at 0°C or it can be high like that of sugar.

Notice: The temperature reading of the thermometer does not change much until all the ice has melted. The heat is being used to change the ice into liquid water.

Review Exercise II. C.

1. If we keep heating a solid, it suddenly stops expanding and changes into a
   _____.

2. The temperature at which a change of form occurs, from a solid to a liquid, is
   called the _____.

Melting Ice in Nature

III. Liquids

Liquids are substances that flow freely like water.

A. Liquid Matter

Liquids have two characteristics:

1. Liquids have no definite shape.

When you place some water in an empty glass, the water spreads out. The mass of water takes the shape of the glass. If you poured the water into a jar, the water would take the shape of the jar. However, if you placed solid cubes of ice in the glass, the cubes would remain the shape of cubes.

2. Liquids have a definite volume.

The water you poured into the glass does not expand to completely fill the glass into which it is poured, like a gas. Neither can you completely empty a big jar of water into a small container. You will have a great deal of water left over, or running over. So the mass of water takes up a definite amount of space. Water is said to have a definite volume.

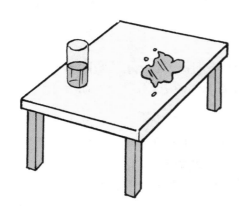

Water spreads out to fill the container into which it is put because it is liquid and not a solid.

The water in a glass does not spread through the air in a room because it is a liquid. The vapor of perfume will spread out because it is a gas.

 Review Exercise III. A.

1. Liquids are characterized by two characteristics:

    a. They have no definite _____.

    b. They have a definite _____.

2. Solids have a definite _____ and a definite volume.

3. Cubes of ice differ from water in that they have _____.

B. Liquids and Temperature

When we increase the temperature of a liquid by heating it, we find that its volume gets larger. This is called thermal expansion. The amount of expansion a liquid undergoes depends on the type of liquid.

 Practical Application: Learn the effects of the thermal expansion of water.

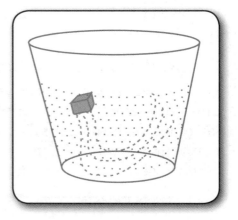

Materials: blue food coloring, cold water, hot water, a refrigerator freezer, an ice tray, and a spoon

Step 1: Add several drops of blue food coloring to a glass of cold water that is three quarters full. Stir the colored water with a spoon.

Step 2: Pour the colored water in an ice tray. Place the ice tray in the freezer and wait several hours until the colored water is frozen.

Step 3: Fill a glass three quarters full with hot water from the sink faucet. Place the glass on a table.

Step 4: Remove a colored ice cube from the tray in the freezer. Add the colored ice cube to the hot water. Describe what happens to the color in the glass.

In this experiment, the hot water in the glass is warmer than the colored water that forms when the ice cube is melted. Because of thermal expansion, a pound of hot water takes up more volume than a pound of cold water. So cold water is more dense than hot water. This is why the streams of colored water from the ice cube sink to the bottom of the glass of hot water; being more dense, the colored water is heavier.

Notice that the falling cold water pushes the hot water out of its way. This sets up water currents in the glass. This is why some colored water moves back to the top of the glass. This movement of water due to differences in temperature is called convection.

Do you remember that convection is one of the causes of the currents in the ocean? Convection also is the reason why the water in a pot on the stove gets hot everywhere in the pot, even though the pot is heated only at the bottom.

Review Exercise III. B.

1. When we increase the temperature of a liquid by heating it, we find it undergoes thermal _____.

2. This movement of water due to differences in temperature is called _____.

3. Convection is one of the causes of the currents in the _____.

C. Solids, Liquids, and Gases

Most liquids when cooled to a very low temperature will become solids. This change of form is called freezing. The temperature at which this occurs is called the freezing point. The actual temperature of the freezing point varies with the particular substance. It can be very high or very low. It is the same temperature as the melting point of the solid. So solid ice melts and becomes water at 0° C, and water freezes and becomes a solid at 0° C.

If you keep heating a liquid, it suddenly stops expanding and slowly changes to a gas. We see steam rising from the boiling water, and the amount of water in the pan decreases. This change of form is called boiling and the temperature at which this occurs is called the boiling point. Water boils at 100° C.

As the liquid is boiled, heat is absorbed by the liquid. Again it will surprise you, but the temperature of the substance does not change. The ongoing heat is being used to convert the liquid into a gas, so the turned up heat does not raise the temperature of the liquid but rather converts the liquid to steam more quickly. When you see a pot of water boil on the stove, the water is being turned into water vapor [a gas] throughout the liquid. The "boiling" is the bubbles of water vapor escaping in the form of steam.

Have you noticed what happens to most liquids left open to the air for a day or two? Most liquids left exposed to the open air over time, slowly change to a gas and the substance "disappears" from the open container. This process is called evaporation. How many times do you leave a glass of water on the table, and when you observe it the next day, there is less water in the glass due to evaporation. That happens because water absorbs heat from the atmosphere to change to a gas. It is a process different from boiling because no heat is added to the liquid.

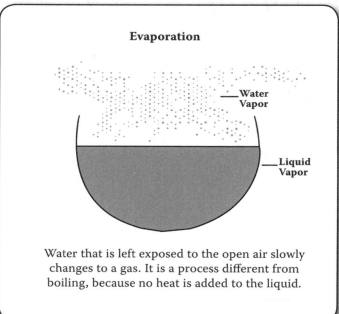

Evaporation

Water Vapor

Liquid Vapor

Water that is left exposed to the open air slowly changes to a gas. It is a process different from boiling, because no heat is added to the liquid.

Practical Application: Learn that the freezing points of substances are different.

Materials: peanut oil, sunflower oil, two small paper cups, a measuring cup, a felt pen, a freezer

Step 1: Using the felt pen, label one paper cup "peanut oil" and the other "sunflower oil."

Step 2: Pour one-third cup of peanut oil in the cup labeled "peanut oil" and one-third cup of sunflower oil in the cup labeled "sunflower oil".

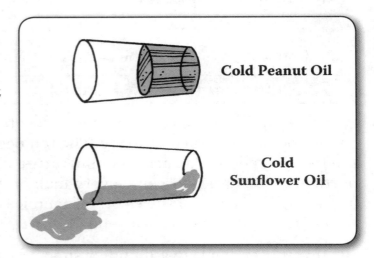

Cold Peanut Oil

Cold Sunflower Oil

Step 3: Place the two cups of oil in the freezer. Leave them overnight.

Step 4: Remove the two cups of oil from the freezer.

Has the peanut oil become a solid? _____

Has the sunflower oil become a solid? _____

What happens when you let the cups stand on the table for several hours?

_____

Note: Generally the freezer is cold enough to freeze peanut oil but not sunflower oil. You can repeat this experiment with other oils like olive oil, corn oil, soybean oil, and safflower oil.

 Review Exercise III. C.

1. When a liquid is cooled to a low enough temperature to become a solid, we call this change _____.

2. When a liquid is heated to a high enough temperature to become a gas, we call this change _____.

3. _____ happens because liquid absorbs heat from the atmosphere to change to a gas.

D. The Uniqueness of Water

Water is a liquid but water is also a primary component of all living matter. Water is odorless and tasteless.

Water is a very remarkable substance. It has a very special characteristic in that liquid water is heavier than ice, or solid "water."

Most substances become bigger (expand) when they are heated and become smaller (contract) when they are cooled. This is true of most substances whether they are solids, liquids, or gases; so generally, a solid is heavier than a liquid and a liquid is heavier than a gas.

Water does not follow this usual pattern! As water cools down, it also begins to contract as its components move closer together. Then, at about 3° C, just before the temperature of the water gets cold enough for it to become ice, water stops contracting and begins to become larger as it cools further. Thus, when water becomes ice at 0° C, the ice solid is lighter than liquid water. So one cup of ice weighs less than one cup of water!

On a very cold day, the water on top of a pond freezes and becomes ice. If water behaved as other liquids, ice would be heavier than water, and would sink to the bottom of the pond, gradually filling up the pond with ice, and giving the fish [and other creatures] who live there no place to live. Interestingly, because the ice is lighter in weight than water, ice floats on top of the pond, leaving room below for fish and plants to live in the water. Ice actually insulates or protects the lower part of the pond from any further drops in cold temperatures.

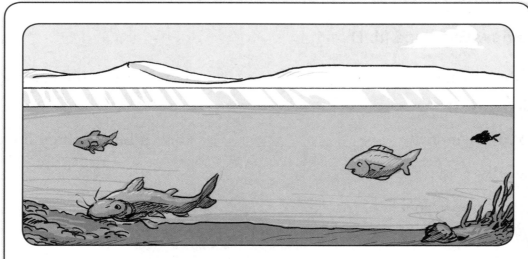

Ice floats on water because it expands when it reaches the freezing point. The ice on top of a pond helps protect water plants and fish during the cold weather. They live beneath the ice until it melts in warmer weather.

Scientists have found that this unique property of water is related to a special feature of the way hydrogen and oxygen fit together. Let us praise and thank Almighty God who created water with this special property.

 Practical Application: Study the strange behavior of water's volume.

Caution: Parental supervision needed

Materials: glass jar, pot, electric stove, refrigerator, cardboard (to cover the top of the jar), two ice cubes, and a glass of water

Step 1: Fill a jar to the brim with water. Heat the jar with water gently in a pot containing about two inches of water.

You will see: The water overflows the jar as it is heated. This is because water, like other liquids, expands when heated. So it takes up more space.

Step 2: Allow the jar to cool and fill it once again to the brim. Place it in the refrigerator to cool overnight.

You will see: The jar is no longer full. This is because water contracts, as it gets cooler, so it takes up less space.

Step 3: Place the piece of cardboard on the jar of cold water. Place the jar in the freezer of your refrigerator overnight.

You will see: The cardboard cap is forced off. This is because water, as it cools below 3 °C to its freezing point, expands. So ice takes up more space than the water it comes from.

 Review Exercise III. D.

1. Most substances _____ when heated, and contract when cooled.

2. A solid is generally _____ than a liquid and a liquid is generally heavier than a _____.

3. When water becomes ice at _____°C, this solid ice is _____ than water.

4. Because ice is _____ than water, it _____ on top of a pond.

5. Ice protects or _____ a pond from further cold temperatures.

IV. Gases

Gas is a substance that has no definite shape or volume, but tends to expand indefinitely.

A. Gaseous Matter

Gases have two important properties.

1.   Gases have no definite shape.

When you put some gas, such as air, in an empty balloon, the air spreads out and takes the shape of the balloon.

2.   Gases have no definite volume.

Air, or any gas, expands to fill any container into which it is pumped, whether it be a small balloon or large balloon. If you push hard enough, you can make a gas fill any size container.

When a gas fills a container, it exerts a force on the walls of the container. This pressing of a gas on the walls of a container is called pressure. It is air pressure that keeps a balloon filled out. It is air pressure in huge tires that holds up the weight of a big truck on its tires.

 Practical Application: Show that air has weight.

Materials: transparent tape, pencil, stick (no shorter than 2 feet in length), three balloons of same size, 4 pieces of string (each one foot in length)

Step 1: Use the transparent tape to secure the end of the pencil to the edge of a table.

Step 2: Tie one of the strings around the center of the stick. Loop the free ends around the pencil and then tie them. The stick will now be suspended from the pencil. Adjust the position of the string in order to balance the stick.

Step 3: Use two pieces of string to suspend two uninflated balloons from the stick an equal distance from the support string. Move the balloons back and forth until the yardstick and the balloons balance.

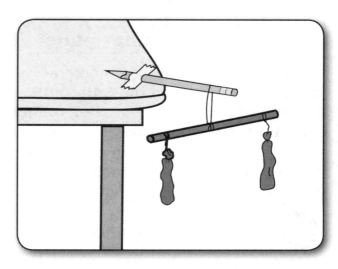

Step 4: Remove one of the uninflated balloons and replace it with an inflated balloon.

The experiment shows that air is matter, even though we cannot see it. We can see the results of the pressure of air or any gas. We know that air has weight because the filled balloon weighs more than an empty balloon. Air is a gas. Air is not a solid because it has no definite shape. Air is not a liquid because air occupies no definite volume.

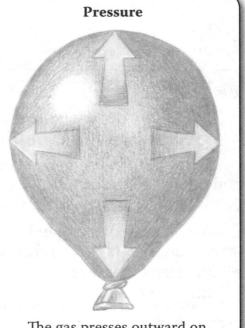

Pressure

The gas presses outward on the walls of its container. This pressing is called pressure.

 Review Exercise IV. A.

1. Gases have no definite _____ and no definite _____.

2. _____ is the pressing of a gas on the walls of a container.

B. Gases and Temperature

When we increase the temperature of a gas by heating it, we find that the pressure of the gas on the walls of the container increases. This is because the gas expands to occupy a greater volume due to thermal or heat expansion. If we decrease the temperature of the gas, then the pressure decreases. Usually, the same amount of any gas in a container will expand about the same volume when heated. This is different from solids or liquids, where the amount of thermal expansion depends on the material itself.

 Practical Application: See that a gas expands when heated.

Materials: an empty soft drink bottle (glass or plastic), a quarter, a refrigerator freezer, a few drops of water

Step 1: Place the empty uncapped bottle in the refrigerator freezer.

Step 2: Wait ten minutes and then remove it from the freezer and place it on a table or other flat surface.

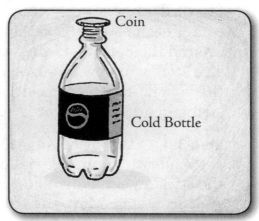

Coin

Cold Bottle

Step 3: Wet your finger and spread water across the quarter and around the top of the bottle. Slip the quarter on the bottle top, making sure the quarter covers the mouth of the bottle.

Step 4: Watch the quarter for several minutes, listening for any sounds.

In this experiment, the air inside the bottle is chilled when the bottle is placed in the freezer. When you take the bottle out of the freezer, the cold air begins to heat up and to expand. As the air warms even more, the air pushes harder on the walls of the bottle container. Finally, the air pushes hard enough to raise the quarter and let some of the air escape. You can hear a click as the air rushes out. As the air continues to warm inside the bottle, the quarter may jump several times.

 Review Exercise IV. B.

1. When we increase the temperature of a gas by heating it, we find that the _____ of the gas on the walls of the container increases.

2. Usually if there is the same amount of any gas in a container, then the amount by which it expands when heated is about the _____ amount or volume.

3. When heat is applied to solids and liquids, however, the amount of expansion depends on the type of _____, such as wood or concrete.

C. Gases and Liquids

When gases are cooled to a low enough temperature, the gases will become liquids. This change of form is called condensation. The temperature at which this occurs is called the condensation point for that gas. The actual temperature of the condensation point varies with the particular gas or material. The condensation point can be very low, like that of air. The condensation point can be very high, like that of water vapor. In the previous chapter, we saw that the condensation point of water determines the kind of weather we will have.

If we keep heating a gas, it continues to expand and thus increases the pressure on the walls of its container. If the gas is heated to a high enough temperature, the gas can exert enough pressure to actually explode the container! If a gas is heated to extremely high temperatures, like that at the center of the Sun, it suddenly stops expanding and slowly changes to a very different form!

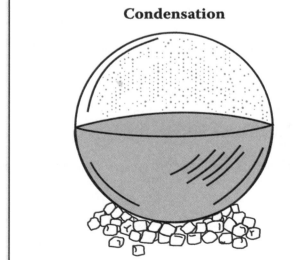

Condensation

When a gas is cooled to a low enough temperature, condensation occurs.

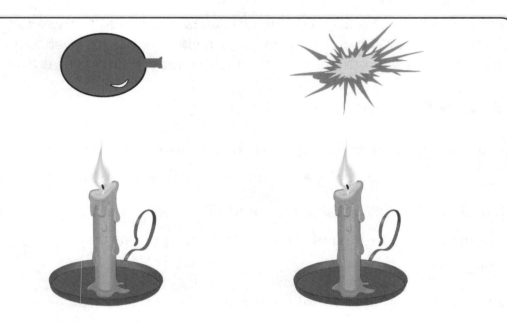

If a gas is heated to an extremely high temperature,
then the pressure will increase so much that the container will explode.

Review Exercise IV. C.

1. When a gas is cooled to a low enough temperature, it will become a _____.

2. _____ is what we call the process when a gas cools and becomes liquid.

3. The actual _____ of the condensation point varies with the particular material.

4. If a gas in heated to an extremely high temperature, the gas pressure will _____ the container!

Review for Chapter Four

Matter: Solids, Liquids, Gases

True or False. Please mark "T" for true or "F" for false.

_____ 1. All material things are solids.

_____ 2. All material things have volume.

_____ 3. When you heat a solid, it expands.

_____ 4. When you cool a solid, it changes to a liquid.

_____ 5. When you heat a liquid, it changes to a gas.

Please match the words on the left with the correct sentence on the right.

_____ 6. God   a. have no definite shape.

_____ 7. Marie Curie   b. is a pressing or force on the walls of a container.

_____ 8. liquids   c. discovered polonium and radium.

_____ 9. melting   d. is pure Spirit.

_____ 10. pressure   e. is a change from a solid to a liquid.

Please complete the sentences.

11. Satellites in orbit have the same mass but lighter _____ than on planet Earth.

12. Whether a thing is found as a solid or liquid or gas depends on its _____.

13. Solids have a definite volume and a definite _____.

14. When you increase the temperature of a liquid by heating it, you find that its _____ gets larger.

15. Evaporation is different from boiling because you add no heat, yet the liquid changes to a _____ over a period of time.

Circle the correct answer.

16. Unlike most materials, solid water is _____ than liquid water.

    a) heavier   b) lighter   c) no different

17. Gases have:

    a) definite shape and size

    b) definite shape but no definite size

    c) no definite shape but definite size

    d) no definite shape and no definite size

18. Thermal expansion occurs in:

    a) solids only

    b) solids and liquids only

    c) liquids and gases only

    d) solids and liquids and gases

19. Material things :

    a) can be everywhere

    b) are all liquids

    c) always have weight

    d) can be seen, touched, tasted, and smelled

20. Water is found as ice when its temperature is

    a) above 100 °C

    b) between 100 °C and 3°C

    c) between 3 °C and 0 °C

    d) below 0 °C.

Chapter Five: Machines

> "But the Lord is the true God . . . He that makes the Earth by His Power, and prepares the world by His wisdom, and stretches out the heavens by His knowledge."
>
> **Jer. 10:10, 12**

Introduction

Machines are things invented to make life easier for people to accomplish their work. Machines are invented so less energy is needed by people and more energy is done by the invention. For instance, a sewing machine means a person does not need to take each little stitch by hand; the machine sews many stitches a hundred times more quickly than a person could do it. Today, most young people do not even know about the machine called a typewriter because now we have computers and keyboards. The invention of machines, such as the automobile and the airplane, are two more examples of how the invention of machines has changed the lives of everyone in the whole world.

Leonardo da Vinci was an Italian Catholic who lived from 1452 to 1519, the period of time when Christopher Columbus was exploring the oceans. Leonardo da Vinci was an outstanding scientist and engineer, and was very informed about the discoveries of the explorers of that time. He is known as a famous painter, a great sculptor, a poet, and a musician. Leonardo painted probably the most famous paintings in the world, *The Last Supper* and the *Mona Lisa*.

Leonardo da Vinci was actually a great genius in so many areas that many believe he was given special blessings from God. One area which impresses us all even today is that of his inventions, or ideas of inventions. He invented the wheelbarrow, the tank, and ball bearings. He drew plans or illustrations for dozens of machines and even experimented with models of airplanes and submarines. As an engineer, he made designs for bridges that were centuries ahead of his time. As a scientist, his notebooks carry records of his research into how the human body and the laws of nature work. Leonardo da Vinci is certainly someone who is a hero among those interested in machines.

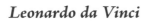

Leonardo da Vinci

Review Exercise

1. Machines are things invented by people to help people accomplish their
   _____.

2. With machines, less _____ is needed by people.

3. Name a machine in your home that helps someone do less work.
   _____

4. Leonardo da Vinci was considered a great _____ because he
   thought of so many inventions.

5. Da Vinci was a great inventor who experimented with models of airplanes
   and _____.

6. Da Vinci was a great scientist who researched the workings of the human
   body and the laws of _____.

7. Da Vinci was also a very talented poet, _____, and sculptor.

Last Supper by Leonardo da Vinci

Outline of Chapter Five

I. Force
   A. Providing Forces
   B. Examples of Motion
      1. Walking on Land
      2. Swimming in Water
      3. Flying in Air
      4. Traveling in Space
II. The Power of Machines
   A. What Machines Do
   B. Machines and Nature
      1. Water
      2. Wind
      3. Sun
III. Turbines and Engines
   A. Steam and Gas Turbines
   B. Engines
IV. Magnetism and Electricity
   A. Magnets
   B. Electromagnetism
   C. Electric Motors
   D. Electric Generators

Chapter Aims

1. understand a little about the principles of motion
2. know what machines do
3. know how some simple machines work
4. know how magnets behave
5. know how electricity is produced and why it is so useful

Activities

1. Observe things in motion.
2. Observe that the air rushing over a wing pushes it upwards.
3. Observe the usefulness of a lever.
4. Make a waterwheel and windmill.
5. Learn how a steam turbine works.
6. Explore the world of magnets.
7. Learn that an electric current produces a magnetic field.
8. Generate electricity.

I. Force

A force is the strength or energy that is applied to something to cause motion or change.

 Practical Application: Observe things in motion.

Materials: balloon, 3 inch square of heavy cardboard, empty sewing spool, glue, point of a ball-point pen to make an "air car" without wheels

Step 1: Make a hole with the ball point pen in the very center of the square of heavy cardboard. Begin the hole on the smooth side.

Step 2: Glue one end of the empty spool to the rough side of the square of cardboard. Be sure that the hole in the spool is directly over the hole in the cardboard.

Step 3: When the glue is completely dry, attach the balloon to the spool and place the "air car" on a flat surface. Give the air car a push. Notice how far the car moves.

Step 4: Inflate the balloon and re-attach it to the spool. Air will now come out from beneath the cardboard to provide a thin space of air between the cardboard and counter. Give the car a push. Notice how it moves with no sign of slowing down, until the balloon is deflated again.

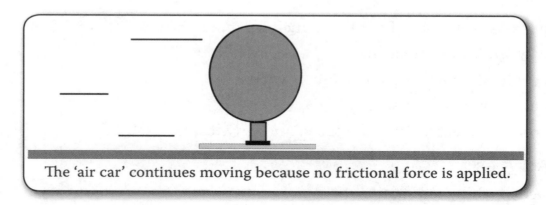

The 'air car' continues moving because no frictional force is applied.

You know that God created all things. In Him, all things move, live, and have their being. Scientists have discovered that there are three principles which God has willed all moving things to obey.

1. Force moves things.

2. Mass has its own resistance.

3. Motion requires force and resistance.

A. Providing Forces

1. In order to make something start to move, stop moving, or turn, a force must be provided.

In our experiment, the "air car" was slowed quickly by the force of friction when the balloon was not inflated. When the balloon was inflated, the thin layer of air prevented the frictional force from being applied, so the "air car" continued in its motion unchanged. When you turn your bicycle into the driveway, you are providing the force which twists the handle bars and causes the turn. We have learned already about one of the greatest forces in a previous chapter. You learned that it is the force of gravity that turns the planets around the Sun.

2. Something cannot move if the resistance is too much for the force.

As we noted before, all matter has its own resistance to a force and this is called its mass. So, if a stone has too much mass, we are not able to move it by simply using our own muscles; we need help from a friend or machine in order to push it with a greater force. Also, if you are trying to push something uphill, or

if you are trying to push something on a rough surface, this will be very hard to move. Here the forces of **gravity** or friction are resisting our pushing efforts.

3. You cannot make something move unless the force you are using has something to push against.

For example, we are not able to walk if the sidewalk is very slippery. Our feet are not able to push against the slippery surface of the walkway in order to move us forward. Astronauts on a space shuttle are not able to push a satellite with their arms unless they have their feet attached to the spacecraft, so they can push against it. When you ride your bike, what do the pedals move against which makes the wheels move?

The scientist, or student-scientist, who sees an object begin to move, to stop, or to turn, asks the questions:

Where does the force come from?

Against what is the force pushing?

What is the resistance of this object?

These questions are one of the ways God indicates to people that He exists. If you keep asking yourself "Why?" then there is no other answer than that God is the ultimate reason for everything. He is the Unmoved Mover. True scientists understand that without God, there would be no existing world for them to study.

Review Exercise I. A.

1. A _____ must be provided in order to make something begin moving, stop moving, or turn.

2. If a stone has too much _____ , we are not able to move it by simply using our own muscles.

3. You can't make something move unless the force you are using has something to push _____.

4. The three questions that a scientist asks when he sees an object begin to move are:

   "Where does the _____ come from?"

   "Against what is the force _____?"

   "What is the _____ of this object?"

B. Examples of Motion

1. Walking on Land

You walk by pushing on the ground with your feet. The force comes from the muscles in your legs. The more you push with your muscles, the faster you go. The resistance is the weight of your own body. If you are light, then you can walk fast very easily, but if you are heavy, then it takes more effort to walk. This is why little kids can move so much faster than adults!

2. Swimming in Water

We swim by pushing our arms against the water. The force comes from the muscles in our arms and legs. The resistance is the *tug on our bodies* caused by the collisions with the water as it slides by us.

3. Flying in Air

An airplane can fly because the force from the jet engine pushes it forward and the air rushing over the wings pushes the plane upwards. The resistance to the force of the jet engine is the tug of the air on the airplane caused by the air as it slides by. The resistance to the force on the wings pushing the plane upward is the weight of the airplane.

The force on the wings pushing the plane upward depends on how fast the plane is moving. When the airplane is taking off, it must increase its speed quickly. The force on the wings pushing the plane upward is greater than the **weight** of the airplane, so the plane moves upwards.

4. Traveling in Space

Have you wondered how a rocket moves through the vacuum of space? A rocket moves because of the force exerted by the exhaust gases of the rocket engine. The gases push against the rocket as they leave the engine. The gases go in one direction while the rocket goes in another direction. The resistance is the mass of the rocket. The mass is the quantity of matter in the rocket.

 Practical Application: Observe that the air rushing over a wing pushes it upwards.

Materials: piece of paper about 3" by 7", scotch tape, table, and straw

Step 1: Fold the piece of paper so that one side is a little longer than the other. With the longer piece over the shorter one, tape the ends together so that the top is curved.

Step 2: Tape this section of an "airplane wing" to the edge of a table or counter.

Step 3: Blow gently against the front edge of the wing with a soda straw. Notice what happens.

Step 4: Try blowing harder and notice what happens. The air moving over the top of the wing moves faster than the air flowing underneath. This causes a difference in air pressure exerted on the top and bottom of the wing which results in an upwards force.

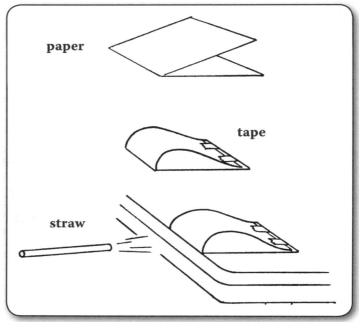

paper

tape

straw

St. Joseph of Cupertino, Patron of Aviators, pray for us.

An aviator is a person who pilots an airplane. The life of St. Joseph of Cupertino, the "Patron of Aviators," reminds us that there are many things in the universe that we do not understand. Even something as simple as the motion of things can be hard to understand. Be sure to ask his help if you are having problems with this chapter. Did you know that St. Joseph of Cupertino is also the patron saint of test-takers?

St. Joseph of Cupertino was born in 1603. His life was marked with many miraculous travels. Those who studied these experiences could find no force present nor any material resistance; there was not anything being pushed against when the saint moved. For example, when he was offering Mass, he frequently floated in the air. On one occasion, he moved through the air carrying a heavy cross that workmen needed to put in place on a wall.

At the end of this earthly world, when we receive miraculous bodies, we will be able to travel in heaven without the need of physical force.

Review Exercise I. B.

1. When you are walking on land, the force comes from the _____ in your legs; the force pushes against the _____ with the front of your feet; the resistance is the _____ of your own body.

2. When you are swimming, the force comes from the _____ in your arms and legs; the force pushes against the _____; the resistance is the tug on your body by the collisions of your body with the _____ as it slides by.

3. When a plane flies, the force comes from the jet _____; the force pushes against the _____, and the airplane; the resistance to the force of the engine is the tug of the air on the _____; the resistance to the force pushing the wings up is the _____ of the plane.

4. When a rocket is sent into space, the force comes from the _____ gases of the rocket engine; the force pushes against the _____ as the gases leave the engine; the resistance is the _____ of the rocket.

5. Who is the saint known as the "Patron of Aviators"? _____

_____

II. The Power of Machines

A machine is a device for performing a task where force or power or energy is needed. A machine is any thing made by man that exerts a force. A machine can be very simple or very complex. A lever is an example of a very simple machine.

A. What Machines Do

 Practical Application: Observe the usefulness of a lever.

Materials: four books, two pencils

Step 1: Stack the books, one on top of the other.

Step 2: Put your finger under the edge of the bottom book of the stack and try to lift the books.

Step 3: Place a ruler under the edge of the bottom book in the stack. Place the pencil under the ruler near the book. The ruler and pencil now form a simple machine called a lever.

Step 4: Push down on the end of the ruler with your little finger and try to lift the books. Notice how easy it is to lift the books. Notice also how far you push the pencil and how far the books rise.

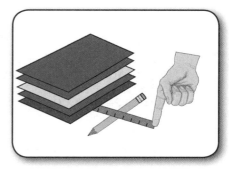

Step 5: Move the pencil under the ruler a little away from the books and again try to lift the books. Notice how easy it is and how far you can raise the books with the pencil lever.

Since machines can provide a much greater force or power than any man by himself could provide, machines make our lives much easier. There are at least three things that machines can do to help people.

1. Machines can transfer force from one place to another.

What happens with a simple machine like the lever we made in our experiment?

The force exerted by your hand is transferred to the pile of books. A similar thing happens in simple machines like bottle openers and hammers.

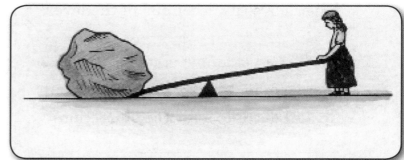

2. Machines can increase the strength or amount of a force.

What happens in our experiment when we use the ruler lever to move the stack of books? The ruler lever transfers the small pushing force of our finger to the stack. The ruler lever makes the pushing force much stronger than the push of our finger. There is an increase of the strength in the push of the ruler lever on the stack as we move the pencil closer to the stack. When using the lever, the end which pushes up on the stack does not move as far as the end we push down on.

On this Earth, we need physical force to be able to move things. God, in His love for mankind, shows us in His saints like St. Joseph of Cupertino, that we won't need physical force in Heaven.

3. Machines can change the direction of a force.

In our experiment with the lever, we saw that our downwards push was changed into an upwards push by the lever machine. Similarly, when you pedal a bicycle, the force of your legs pumping up and down is changed into a force that pushes the bicycle forward.

Review Exercise II. A.

1. A machine is a device for performing a task where _____ or power or energy is needed.

2. What is an example of a simple machine that transfers a force from one place to another? _____

3. A machine can increase the size or _____ of a force.

4. The increased push of the lever on the stack of books is gained at the expense of the _____ which we must move the other end of the lever.

5. What is an example of a machine that changes the direction of a force from up and down to a forward direction?

_____

B. Machines and Nature: Water, Wind, Sun

A force must be used to make a machine work. Long ago, the forces needed to make machines work were provided mainly by human muscles. Then people found they could use animals to work for them, and provide the forces needed to make machines work. So the forces were provided by the muscles of tame animals like horses, donkeys, and oxen. However, animal muscles get tired after a while. They cannot keep pushing and pulling all day with the same strength of force. So people looked for better ways of providing the forces needed to make machines work. They began to use the various forces found in nature. Two of the most common forces in nature are those of moving water and moving wind. The waterwheel and the windmill are two machines that capture these forces to provide energy or work.

1. Waterwheels: Capturing the Force of Water

Rivers flow from high places to low places. The constantly moving water in a river is subject to the force of gravity when it flows from high places to lower places on the surface of planet Earth. Because of this, moving water in a river has plenty of force to be able to move things. A good-sized river can provide such force over a very long period of time.

For a long, long time, flowing water has been used to provide the force needed to drive machines. The waterwheel is an invention that is used to provide force. The force of the moving water pushes against the blades of the waterwheel, causing it to turn. This turning force is then used to drive other machines that can lift things, or pump water, or grind grain, or make electricity, or do just about anything else that needs the application of a force to move.

2. Windmills: Capturing the Force of Wind

We know that wind is air that is moving, sometimes slowly, other times very fast. We have learned that it is the Sun's energy that causes the wind to move. When the wind moves, it is able to exert a force on another object, simply by pushing on it. Unlike water, however, the wind is not constant and is not as reliable as a waterwheel.

The windmill is an invention that is used to provide force. In this case, the wind pushes the blades of a windmill, causing the blades to turn. This turning force is then used to drive other machines. The force exerted by the wind can be used to lift things, grind grain, pump water, or generate electricity, or do just about anything else that needs the application of a force to move.

 Practical Application: Make a waterwheel and a windmill.

Materials: empty one-half gallon milk carton, pencil (about 7 inches long), pair of scissors, small stone, string, waterproof glue, water faucet

Step 1: Using a milk carton, cut out a circle about 3 inches in diameter. With a pencil, draw lines dividing the circle into four equal parts. In the center of the cut-out circle, draw another circle about 1 inch in diameter.

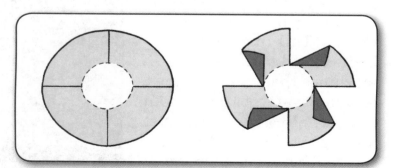

Step 2: Cut along the four lines up to the small circle. Bend the cut part back a little less than halfway.

Step 3: Cut a section out of the milk carton across its width about one-half inch deep and one-half inch wide so that the pencil can sit in it.

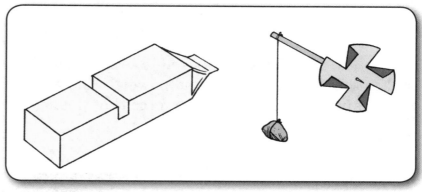

Step 4: Push one end of the pencil through the center of the water wheel to serve as a shaft. Tie the piece of string to the small stone and the other end of the string to the end of the pencil opposite from the waterwheel. Put a dab of glue to hold the waterwheel in place on the pencil. Place the pencil shaft in the section cut out of the carton.

Step 5: Hold the milk carton so that the wheel is in a thin stream of water. The wheel turns, the shaft turns, and the thread winds up and lifts the stone.

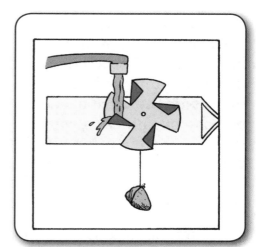

Step 6: Now use a larger stream of water against the blades. With more force, the stone will be lifted faster. You have provided an invention of force by means of a waterwheel.

Step 7: Remove the wheel from the water and blow on the blades. Can you blow hard enough to make the wheel turn and lift the stone? You have provided the equivalent of a windmill which can provide a force needed to move things.

3. Using the Wind

We know that wind is moving air. In a previous chapter, we learned that it is the Sun's energy that causes the wind to move in the atmosphere. Anything that is moving is able to exert a force on another object simply by pushing upon it.

As you travel, be sure to look about and see if you can see any windmills or wind turbines. You can find wind turbines on some farms as they are sometimes used to pump water from a well into the fields to water the crops. Some communities have been investing in wind turbines to provide electricity. There are probably about one million homes which have electricity provided by wind turbines.

Several states, such as Washington, Iowa, Texas, California, and Minnesota, have a number of wind turbines or wind machines producing electricity for homes.

On the sea, the wind is used to provide the force needed to move ships. The sail makes the ship move by "wind power." The wind pushes on the sail and this in turn transfers this force into a force that pushes the ship forward.

4. Using the Water

Rivers flow from high places to low places. It is the force of gravity that causes the water to flow from the high places, where it falls as rain, to the low places of the Earth's surfaces.

"Water wheel" used to provide force

The moving water in a river has plenty of force to move things. For a long time, flowing water has been used to provide the force needed to drive machines. A water wheel or water turbine is often used. Here the moving water pushes against the blades of the wheel, causing it to turn. The force that turns the wheel is then used to drive other machines that lift things, pump water, grind grain, or make electricity for a community.

Some communities are located near a good sized river where there is good rainfall and nearby mountains from which rain runs down into the river. Sometimes a dam is built to hold back the water. This water is then directed through pipes downhill to a water turbine. In turn, these water turbines are connected to generators which distribute electricity to homes and businesses.

5. Using the Sun

The Sun produces great amounts of heat and energy. Man has always known this. However, it was not until recently that ways have been found that can harness this great source of energy. An amazing development has been the invention of the solar panel. Solar panels, often installed on roofs of homes or buildings, are able to collect the Sun's energy, and to provide the needed electrical power to heat homes and electrical appliances.

Even more recent developments are producing solar generators that store the energy collected through solar panels. The battery of the generator is recharged constantly by the rays of the Sun.

Review Exercise II. B.

1. A _____ must be used to make a machine work.

2. Muscles cannot keep pushing and pulling all day with the same _____ of force.

3. The most common forces in nature that we use in order to make machines work are the forces exerted by _____ and _____.

4. Anything that is _____ is able to exert a force.

5. The "machine" used to make a ship move by "wind power" is called a _____.

6. On land, the force exerted by the moving wind is used to grind grain and pump water, as well as to make _____.

7. It is the force of _____ that causes the water to flow from high places to low places on Earth's surface.

III. Turbines and Engines

A turbine is a type of engine that usually contains rotary blades like those on a windmill or waterwheel. Pressure from water, steam, or air must be applied in order to make the blades spin.

A. Steam and Gas Turbines

 Practical Application: Learn how a steam turbine works.

Caution: Parental supervision needed.

Materials: waterwheel/windmill from earlier experiment, a teakettle, a piece of aluminum foil, a rubber band, a pencil, kitchen mittens, heat to boil water

Step 1: Wrap the piece of aluminum foil around the spout of the kettle. Tighten a rubber band around the foil at the bottom. Wrap the upper end of the foil around a pencil. Remove the pencil so that there is now a small opening.

Step 2: Wearing kitchen hot pads or mittens, hold the turbine in front of the steaming kettle, above the opening in the aluminum foil. Watch the waterwheel/windmill/turbine turn.

Just like the moving wind and the moving water, moving steam can be used to provide the force needed to drive a machine. The steam hits the blades of a wheel, called a turbine, making it turn. The hotter the steam, the faster the turbine moves. The faster the steam moves, the more force it will have. The turning force of a turbine often is used to drive other machines.

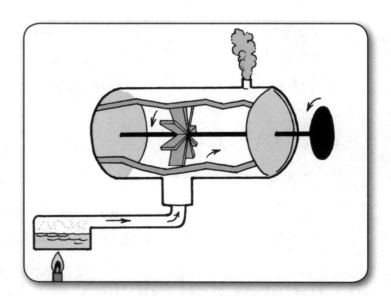

Steam turbines have been used to make heavy locomotives and ships move. Today, steam turbines are used mostly to provide the turning force to make electricity. The heat energy used for making steam from water comes from burning fuels such as coal, oil, wood, or natural gas.

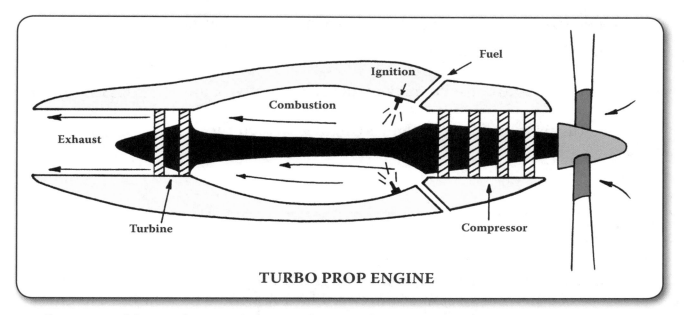

TURBO PROP ENGINE

In gas turbines, the moving gas that pushes the blades of the turbines is produced by burning gasoline or some other liquid fuel. When gasoline or some other liquid fuels burn, they give off very hot gases that have much more force than steam from boiling water.

The very hot gases that are released push against the blades of a turbine and make it rotate very, very quickly. For this reason, gas turbines are used in huge machines, such as trucks, locomotives, and ships. Turbines provide a great enough force needed to make them move. Gas turbines are used also in some airplanes to turn the propellers very very fast.

 Review Exercise III. A.

1. Just like the wind, moving steam can be used to provide the _____ needed to drive a machine.

2. The steam hits the blades of a wheel, called a _____, making it turn.

3. The _____ force of a turbine is used to drive other machines.

4. The heat energy used for making _____ from water comes from burning fuels such as coal, oil, wood, or natural gas.

5. In gas turbines, the moving gas that pushes against the blades of the turbine is produced by burning _____ or some other fuel.

6. When gasoline burns, it gives off very hot gases that have much _____ force than steam from boiling water.

7. Gas turbines are used to make trucks, locomotives, and _____ move.

8. Gas turbines are used in some airplanes to turn the _____ very very fast.

B. Engines

A machine that uses the force exerted by a hot gas is called an engine. Engines are very useful because they can be used anywhere. People don't need to rely on the presence of a flowing stream of water or blowing wind when they use engines.

In an engine, the fuel is allowed to burn in a special container called a cylinder. It is called a cylinder because it has the shape of a cylinder. One of the cylinder's round ends, called a piston, is free to slide. One end of a rod is then attached to the piston and the other is attached to a bent piece of metal, called a crankshaft. The crankshaft is then attached to a wheel.

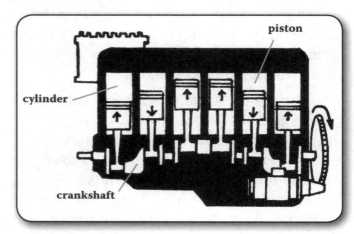

When the fuel is burned inside the cylinder, the molecules of heated air and gas push the piston downward; this then pushes the rod; the rod turns the crankshaft and thus, the wheel is turned. The engine uses the force of a heated gas to turn the wheel.

The gasoline engine in a car, bus, or plane uses a fuel called gasoline. It comes from the crude oil which is pumped out of the oil wells.

Some engines in trucks, trains, and boats burn oil instead of gasoline. These engines are called diesel engines because they use diesel fuel. Diesel engines are much like gasoline engines, but they are much better at pulling heavy loads. Diesel fuel expands more slowly than gasoline; therefore, it provides a slow but steady push, while gasoline provides a series of bursts.

Review Exercise III. B.

1. What is a machine that uses the force exerted by a hot gas? _____

2. What is the name of the special container in an engine where the fuel is burned? _____

3. When the fuel is burned inside the cylinder of an engine, the force moves from a piston to a rod to a crankshaft and then to a _____.

4. A gasoline engine uses _____ as a fuel.

5. What fuel does a diesel engine burn? _____

Pratt & Whitney R-2800-21 Twin Wasp Radial Engine

IV. Magnetism and Electricity

A. Magnets

Magnets are objects that are surrounded by a magnetic field and thus attract pieces of iron or steel. There are many uses for magnets in our daily lives. There are magnetic pens and ashtrays. Magnets are used to hold cupboard and refrigerator doors closed, and to hold messages on display boards.

 Practical Application: Explore the world of magnets.

Materials: a magnetic compass, a magnet (a simple refrigerator magnet will do), some paper clips, small pieces of paper, a small piece of wood

Step 1: Take the magnetic compass and let it rest on the table until the pointer comes to rest.

Step 2: Bring a paper clip close to one end of the compass pointer. Notice what the compass pointer does. Now move the paper clip around the compass and notice what the pointer does. Do the same thing with the piece of paper and wood.

You should observe that the compass pointer is attracted to the paper clip, and not to the paper or wood.

Step 3: Bring one end of the magnet close to the compass pointer and observe what happens.

You should observe that the end of the magnet attracts one end of the compass pointer and repels the other end. So the only things that affect a magnet are pieces of iron and steel and other magnets.

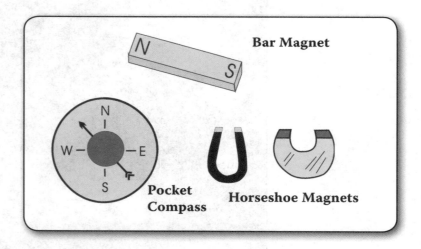

Step 4: Bring one end of the magnet close to the paper clips, the pieces of paper, and the wood. Notice that it attracts only the paper clips.

The magnet behaves exactly as the pointer of the compass, indicating that the compass pointer is a magnet also.

Magnets have been around for a very long time. No one knows how magnets got their name. One story is that they are named after Magnes, a shepherd boy who lived many years ago in ancient Greece. One day, the story goes, he rested his iron tipped crook against a rock and found that it held the crook tight. A rock like this had never been found before. Pieces of it were called magnets.

It is not known if this story of Magnes is true or not. However, there is a kind of rock found in nature that does attract iron and steel. It is known as magnetite or lodestone. Pieces of it are natural magnets. Today, most magnets are made out of special materials and are much stronger than pieces of magnetite.

The ends of a magnet are called its poles. Every magnet has two poles. One is called a "south" pole and the other a "north" pole. These poles are places where the forces of attraction on the piece of iron or steel are the greatest.

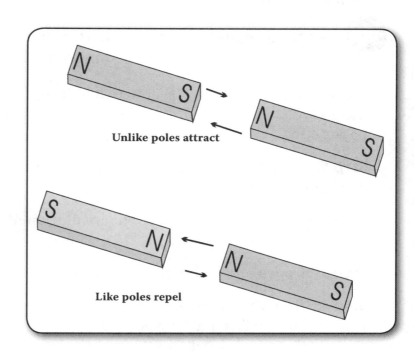

Unlike poles attract

Like poles repel

When the end of one magnet is brought near the end of another magnet, the ends will exert a force on one another. If one of the ends is a south pole and the other is a north pole, they will pull towards one another, or attract each other. If one of the ends is a south pole and the other is also a south pole, they will push away from one another, or repel one another.

Let Christ be your magnet and Mary the force that draws you to Him.

 Review Exercise IV. A.

1. Magnets are objects that _____ pieces of iron or steel.

2. The kind of rock found in nature which attracts iron and steel is called _____ or lodestone.

3. The _____ of a magnet are places where the forces of attraction on the piece of iron or steel are the greatest.

4. If the north pole of one magnet is brought near the south pole of another magnet, the two magnets will _____ one another.

5. If the south pole of one magnet is brought near the south pole of another magnet, the two magnets will _____ one another.

B. Electromagnetism

A device that becomes a magnet when an electric current flows through its wires is called an electromagnet. Today, electromagnets are far more important than magnets found in nature or magnets made by men. Electromagnets are an important part of many electrical devices. If we went on a "magnet" hunt in our homes, we would find electromagnets in doorbells, telephone receivers, radios, television sets, and many other devices that use electricity.

 Practical Application: Learn that an electric current produces a magnetic field.

Materials: 1 yd. of wire (18-gauge, insulated; can be obtained from a hardware store), 1½-volt battery, long iron nail, magnetic compass, and paper clips

Step 1: Wrap the wire tightly around the nail, leaving about 6 inches of free wire at each end.

Step 2: Have an adult remove the insulation about 1 inch from either end of the wire.

Step 3: Secure one end of the wire to one pole of the battery.

Step 4: Place the magnetic compass near the nail and touch the free end of the wire to the free battery pole. Does the compass needle move? When the nail starts to feel warm, disconnect the wire end you are holding from the battery pole.

Step 5: Secure the end of the wire to the other pole of the battery and touch the free end of the wire to the free pole. Does the compass needle move? When the nail starts to feel warm, disconnect the wire end you are holding from the battery pole.

Step 6: Again touch the free end of the wire to the free battery pole, and touch the nail to the pile of paper clips. Lift the nail while keeping the ends of the wire on the paper clip pile.

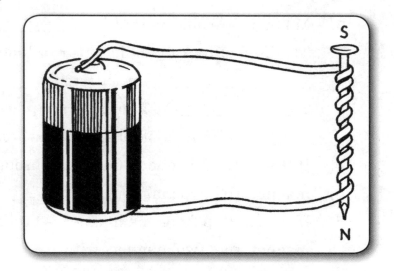

The iron nail has become a magnet because of the influence of the electric current. The electric current exerts magnetic force on another magnet and attracts iron objects.

When the two terminals of a battery are joined by a piece of wire, an electric current flows from the positive terminal to the negative terminal. This moving electric current causes the wire to behave as a magnet. The magnet-wire is able to push or pull on other magnets, and is able to draw nearby pieces of iron or steel to itself.

Review Exercise IV. B.

1. An _____ is a device that become a magnet when an electric current flows through its wires.

2. An electromagnet is an important part of many _____ devices.

3. Where do we find electromagnets in our homes? _____
_____

4. When the two terminals of a battery are joined by a piece of wire, an _____ current flows from the _____ terminal to the negative terminal.

C. Electric Motors

The push or pull produced by an electric current flowing in a wire on nearby magnets, or on pieces of iron or steel, can be used to turn a wheel, just as we use the push of water, steam, or air to turn a wheel. These machines are called electric motors.

Most of the machines that we use in our homes and factories are run by means of electric motors. The use of wind turbines or water turbines is not as convenient or as efficient as that of electric motors. There is less work with electric motors, less effort on the part of people. Electric motors are very small and silent. Electric motors do not need to have a windy day or a river nearby in order to work. Our lives would be very different if we did not have electric motors. If we went on an "electric motor" hunt, we would find that these motors are being used in fans, refrigerators, food processors, vacuum cleaners, even in automobiles.

God has blessed all of us on Earth by showing men how to be more efficient in their daily lives. We need to be sure to thank Him for these blessings.

Review Exercise IV. C.

1. The push or pull produced by an electric current flowing in a wire is used in a special type of machine called an _____ motor.

2. Electric motors are very small and do not need to have a wind or _____ nearby in order to work.

3. Name three items in your home that use electric motors? _____

D. Electric Generators

Michael Faraday was a British physicist. He was a famous inventor who invented and created the first electric generator called the dynamo and the first electric motor.

Michael did not start out as an inventor. Michael Faraday was born into a poor family in London, England, in 1791. The family was too poor to send him to school. When he was fourteen years old, he started working for a bookbinder. As he worked around books, he started reading. He read everything he could find. He especially liked reading about scientific subjects. Michael eventually found a job as a chemical assistant and started learning more about science. That was only the beginning for Michael Faraday. He proved that if anyone wants to learn and to succeed, and to help make life easier for everyone in the world, he must start with reading good books!

Since childhood, most of us have wondered about electric plugs and how they work. Most of the electricity used in homes and factories is not produced by a battery. It comes from a special machine called a generator. When a generator is turned, an electric current begins to flow through attached wires which then are attached to places far away.

The generator can be turned by any one of the machines we have studied so far. In some places, the force of flowing water turns a generator. In other places, it is the force of steam that does the work of turning the generator. Many small generators used on farms producing electricity are turned by gasoline or diesel engines.

It is a great blessing for all of us that the generator does not need to be in the same location as the objects which use the electrical current. We can connect the generator with wires. We now build our factories, homes, and stores anywhere we like, connecting machines and appliances with wires to the electric generator.

 Practical Application: Generate electricity.

Materials: lemon juice, 2 pieces of copper wire (about 6 inch in length), fifteen 1 inch x 1 inch strips of paper towel, 7 copper pennies (dated prior to 1980), 7 nickels or any other coin that is not copper, a rubber band, and a light bulb of less than 1.5 volts (from a flashlight).

Step 1: Soak the paper towel strips in the lemon juice.

Step 2: Make a pile of coins, alternating nickels and pennies. Separate each one with a lemon-soaked strip of paper towel. Bind them together with the rubber band. If you touch each end of the stack with your fingers, you will feel a slight tingle, due to the electric current being generated by your lemon battery.

Step 3: Ask an adult to remove 1 inch of insulation from each end of the pieces of copper wire.

Step 4: Wrap one end of a copper wire around the metal part of the bulb and tuck the other end of it under the rubber band at the dime end of your lemon battery. Tuck one end of the other wire under the penny end of your lemon battery and touch its other end to the metal knob on one end of the bulb. The bulb should light up.

Important Note: In the project to generate electricity, lemon juice was used. The electric current was caused by chemical reactions between the two different metals in the lemon juice. The battery you made is like the ones you buy in the hardware store, except those batteries use different materials.

Review Exercise IV. D.

1. Who is the great inventor of the first electric generator?

   _____ _____

2. How did it happen that Faraday read so many books?

   _____

3. What kind of books did he like to read? _____

4. What was his first scientific job? _____

5. Today, most of the electricity used in homes and factories is not provided by water or steam, gasoline or diesel fuel, or batteries, but by electric

   _____.

6. When a generator is turned, an electric current begins to flow through

   _____ _____which then are attached to places far away.

7. We now build factories, homes, stores anywhere we like because machines and appliances can be _____ by wires to an electric generator far away.

In a hydroelectric dam, it is flowing water
that provides the force to turn the generator.

Review for Chapter Five

Machines

True or False. Please mark "T" for true or "F" for false.

_____ 1. In order to make something begin moving, a force is needed.

_____ 2. A machine increases the amount of a force.

_____ 3. We walk by pushing on the ground with our feet.

_____ 4. Electric motors do not need to have a river nearby to work.

_____ 5. A north pole of a magnet attracts a north pole of another magnet.

Please match the words on the left with the letter of their correct definition.

_____ 6. Joseph of Cupertino   a.   is needed to make something turn,

                                                 begin, or stop moving.

_____ 7. a machine   b.   causes a wire to behave as a magnet.

_____ 8. Leonardo da Vinci   c.   is the patron saint of aviators.

_____ 9. a force   d.   was a great scientist and engineer.

_____ 10. electric current   e.   is a man-made device that exerts a force.

Please complete the sentences below.

11. The three questions that a scientist asks when he sees an object begin to move are:

         "Where does the _____ come from?"

         "Against what is the force _____ ?"

         "What is the_____ of the object?"

12. A _____ must be used to make a machine work.

13. Anything that is _____ is able to exert a force.

14. An _____ is a machine that uses the force exerted by a hot gas.

15. If the north pole of one magnet is brought near the south pole of another, the two magnets will _____.

Circle the letter of the correct answer.

_____ 16. In the case of an airplane, the upward force is provided by
a) the jet engine.   b) the pull of gravity.
c) the air rushing over the wings.   d) the hot air in the cabin.

_____ 17. The increased push of the lever on a stack of books is gained at the expense of
a) the distance we must move the other end.
b) the direction of the force.
c) the pull of gravity.
d) the wind.

_____ 18. Objects that attract pieces of iron or steel are called
a) levers.   b) machines.
c) turbines.   d) magnets.

_____ 19. A machine that uses the push or pull produced by a current flowing in a wire is called
a) a sail.   b) an electromagnet.
c) an electric motor.   d) an engine.

_____ 20. Most of the electricity used in our homes is produced by
a) a battery.   b) a generator.
c) a water wheel.   d) a magnet.

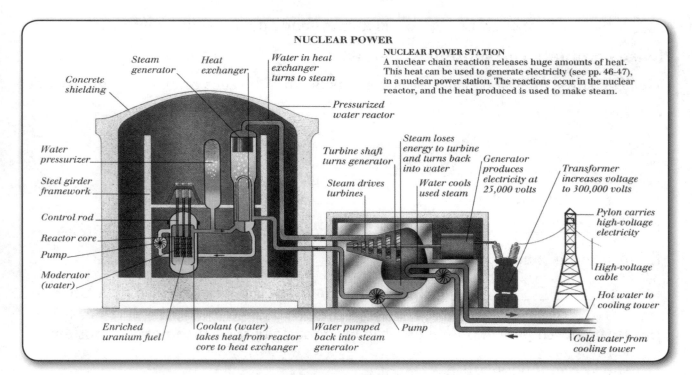

Nuclear power plants provide electricity to many homes.

"And the Earth brought forth the green herb, and such as yieldeth seed according to its kind, and the tree that beareth fruit, having seed each one according to its kind."

Genesis 1:12

Introduction

St. Albert the Great

St. Albert the Great was born in 1206 in a small village in southern Germany. St. Albert became a priest in the Dominican order, which is known for its love of God's truth. He began the task of gathering together human knowledge into an orderly body of knowledge. We would think of it as an encyclopedia. St. Thomas Aquinas was one of his pupils.

In 1260, St. Albert was named a bishop and devoted himself to the duties of his office. Soon he resigned so he could continue his teaching and research. St. Albert died in the city of Cologne, in Germany, in 1280.

St. Albert was a man of great knowledge and learning. He wrote many books on subjects covering many different areas of knowledge, particularly religion and various sciences. He wrote about the stars and planets, he wrote about chemistry, geography, plants, and animals. He wrote about the human body. St. Albert was one of the first persons to recognize that scientists need to study, observe, and write about the world in order to learn and to teach others more about God's laws evident throughout nature. He taught his students that the Source of knowledge and wisdom is the Word of God in the Bible. For these reasons, St. Albert the Great was given the title of patron saint of scientists.

 Review Exercise

1. St. Albert was one of the first to recognize that scientists need to study, to _____, and to write about the world in order to learn God's laws in nature.

2. St. Albert the Great is the Patron Saint of _____.

Outline

I. Living Things
   A. Properties of Living Things
   B. Groups of Living Things

II. The Kingdom of Plants
   A. Introduction
      1. Flowers
      2. Leaves
      3. Stem
      4. Roots
   B. Parts of a Flower
   C. How Flowers Make Seeds

III. The Kingdom of Animals
   A. Introduction
   B. Types of Animals
   C. Insects
   D. Characteristics of Insects
   E. Metamorphosis

IV. The Kingdom of Protists
   A. Introduction
   B. Members of the Protist Kingdom

Bengal Tiger

Chapter Aims

1. know the difference between living and non-living things
2. know the basic groups of living things and what distinguishes them from one another
3. know about the basic parts of a plant and the function of flowers
4. know about the animal and protist kingdoms

Activities

1. see that a plant reacts to things around it
2. study a typical root
3. study the parts of a flower
4. examine the structure of seeds
5. study a typical insect: a grasshopper
6. watch a caterpillar become a moth or butterfly
7. make a water-drop microscope
8. observing members of the protist kingdom

I. Living Things

All living things have certain things in common which we will study in this chapter. To put it simply, living things can grow, they can move, they can reproduce, they can react to things around them. The difference between the non-living and the living things is evident to everyone, even young children. The study of living things is called biology. A scientist who studies living things is called a biologist.

A. Properties of Living Things

Plants, animals, and people are all living things. However, they also are very different from each other. To know if something is alive, we must study them and see what kind of characteristics or properties they possess. Scientists who have studied living things have found that all living things share basic characteristics or properties.

 Practical Application: Observe a plant reacting to things.

Materials: about 4 beans, radish, pumpkin, or sunflower seeds, one small wide-mouth jar, clean absorbent paper, kitchen paper towels, tap water

Step 1: Line the inside of the jar with absorbent paper. Fill the middle of the jar with crumpled paper towels and then saturate the absorbent paper and the towels with water. Pour off the excess water.

Step 2: Push four soaked seeds between the glass and absorbent paper at the top of the jar.

Step 3: In less than a week, the seedlings will begin to grow. After one seedling has grown about an inch above the top of the jar, set the jar on its side.

Step 4: After a few days, examine the seedlings in the jar you have set on its side.

You will observe that the seedlings will have turned on their stems so that they continue to grow upwards. The seedlings have reacted to the direction of the pull of gravity. They always tend to grow upwards away from the center of the Earth and turn their leaves toward the Sun.

Step 5: Set the jar upright and watch as the seedling grows.

Four Basic Properties of Living Things

1. Movement: Living things can move by themselves.

When something moves, it changes its place. All living things move by themselves. Things that are not alive cannot move by themselves. A rock can change its place only if something or someone else moves it. A cat can move from place to place, whenever it wants to.

A plant can open its petals by itself. It can move its leaves toward the sun. Sometimes we cannot see the movement, but it does occur. The petals of a flower open so very slowly that we cannot see them move. However, if we were to watch over a period of several hours, we would notice movement.

2. Reaction: Living things react to things around them.

All living things can sense things around them and they do something because of what they sense. When they do something, we say they react or respond to something around them.

Some living things, such as plants, can sense light and heat. If you place a plant near a window, the plant reacts to the light by bending towards the window. A rock does not react to things around it. A rock does not react to night or day, hot or cold. A rock is not a living thing.

Some special living things sense things around them by means of five special senses: sight, sound, smell, taste, and touch. Animals and humans have this ability.

3. Growth: Living things grow.

All living things get bigger by themselves throughout their life. We call this special God-given gift the ability to grow. A tree grows from an acorn, a dog grows from a puppy, a man grows from a boy. In addition, living things generally repair themselves. If one of the parts of a living thing is lost or worn out, the living thing sometimes will replace the part or repair the injury by itself, for itself. When we get hurt, our body starts to repair itself immediately. The scab which forms immediately on a scratch shows that.

A rock does not grow by itself, nor does it grow a replacement part when part of it is chipped off. A rock is not a living thing.

4. Reproduction: Living things make new living things.

God gives all living things the ability to make new living things just like themselves. We call this special God-given gift the ability to reproduce. Because of this special gift, new living things are being made to "fill the earth" all the time. Cats make kittens. Oak trees make acorns. When God decides to create a new life, people can make children.

 Review Exercise I. A.

1. What are the four basic properties that all living things share?

   _____   _____

   _____   _____

2. When something moves, it changes its _____.

3. When living things sense things around them, they _____.

4. When living things grow, they get bigger by _____.

5. In general, living things _____ themselves when they get hurt.

6. The special gift God gave living things in order to be able "to fill the

   Earth" is the gift of _____.

B. Groups of Living Things

Scientists have grouped all the living things on Earth into kingdoms: Animal, Plant, Protists, Bacteria, and Fungi.

Animals and humans are living things that grow, reproduce, move, and have feeling.

Plants are living things that grow, reproduce, and make their own food.

Protists are living things, such as algae or amoeba, that are not clearly plant or animal.

Bacteria, once called *Monera*, are the simplest and smallest of all life. They reproduce by dividing.

Fungi are plant organisms that rely on dead organisms for food. Fungi include mushrooms, mold, and mildew.

Though scientists include human beings in the Animal category, human beings, people, differ greatly from animals. God made humans in His own image and likeness. In addition to the faculty of reason, God gave each person an immortal everlasting soul, not just a body. Being immortal, the souls of people will live forever. People who love God will live forever in heaven.

At our birth, God gave each of us our own personal Guardian Angel to encourage us and guard us from evil.

God has made another group of living beings, which we cannot see. These living beings are called angels. Like God, they are pure spirit. At our birth, God gave each of us our own personal angel to encourage us and guard us from evil. Let us pray to our guardian angel each day, so that he will help us reach Heaven.

Angel of God, my guardian dear,
To whom God's love commits me here,
Ever this day be at my side,
To light and guard, to rule and guide. Amen.

Review Exercise I. B.

1. Plants are living things that grow, reproduce, and make their own _____.

2. Animals are living things that grow, reproduce, _____, and

   have _____.

3. _____ are living things, such as algae, that are not
   clearly plant or animal.

4. Fungi rely on _____ _____ for food.

5. God made people with souls that live _____.

6. People who love and obey God will live with Him in _____.

7. _____ are the smallest and simplest of all life.

Cup Fungi

II. The Kingdom of Plants

Plants are living things that grow, make their own food, and reproduce.

A. Introduction

 Practical Application: Study a typical root plant.

Materials: three fresh carrots, red vegetable dye (or ink), a glass of tap water, a medicine dropper

Step 1: Cut one carrot across the middle and look at the parts of the carrot closely. Observe that the small roots radiate outwards from the center.

Step 2: Cut another carrot in half lengthwise and look at it closely. Observe that the center core and small roots extend the length of the carrot.

Step 3: Cut the tip off the third carrot and place the cut end in a solution of water containing a dropper full of red vegetable dye. Let it soak for a day. Cut the carrot lengthwise. Look at the colored sections. Observe that the red color in the tubes extends from the tip of the carrot to the top.

Note: The carrot is actually the main root of the carrot plant. It not only stores some food for the plant, but also absorbs water from the soil.

A plant has four main parts: flowers, leaves, stems, and roots. An understanding of each part is necessary in order to see how God has given plants the ability to do what He created them to do.

1. Flowers

The purpose of a flower is to make the seeds from which the new plants grow. Plants can produce only seeds that grow into plants of their own kind. God planned that seeds will be produced when two types of cells produced by the plant join together. This joining together occurs inside flowers.

2. Leaves

There are many different types of leaves, such as oak leaves, cabbage leaves, flower leaves, spinach leaves, and many others. Pine needles and cactus needles are considered leaves.

God made leaves to help the plant grow in many ways. The leaves can shade the roots of the plant as in the case of a tree. The leaves can protect the plant from its enemies as in the case of a cactus. The main purpose of the green leaves of a plant is to make food for the plant.

3. Stem

In God's design, the stem of a plant has two main purposes. The first is to carry water from the roots to the leaves. The second purpose is to carry food from the leaves to the stem and the roots.

Stems are different from one another. Most stems are above the ground and hold the plant up. We are most familiar with the woody stems of trees and shrubs, but other types of stems exist like those that occur in flowering plants. Some stems are below the ground. The potato is a plant whose stem is below the ground.

4. Roots

Roots have many important functions for a plant. The most important job of roots is to hold the plant in place. Roots also hold the soil and dirt of Earth together. Plants, especially trees and bushes, are important and useful for holding the earth or soil together, thereby preventing it from being washed away by rainwater.

Radishes and carrots are two roots that we eat.

Roots are places where the plant can store food. The plant uses this food later. This is why many roots are good to eat as food. Carrots and radishes are roots that we eat. What we are really eating is the food that the plant has stored up for itself.

Another very important job of the root is to soak up minerals and water from the soil. Soil is different from dirt. Dirt is a combination of minerals and small bits of pebbles. Soil is a combination of minerals, decaying plants and animals and insects. Soil contains the life-giving nutrients that plants need to grow. The plant uses minerals and water to make and store food. Most plants absorb water and minerals from the soil through the root hairs that are part of every root.

Some plants do not need soil in order to grow. These plants, such as orchids, have roots that get their food and water from the air. Such plants are often found hanging on trees.

Most plants have several different kinds of roots. The large, main root is called the taproot. It is the first root that grows from the baby plant. Other roots, called branch roots, grow off from the taproot.

 Review Exercise II. A.

1. What is the purpose of a flower? _____

2. What are three ways that leaves help a plant grow? a) to shade the _____ b) to _____ the plant c) to make _____

3. The stem of a plant carries water from the root to the _____.

4. The stem carries food from the leaves to the stem and the _____.

5. What are four functions of the roots of a plant? a) to hold the plant in _____ b) to hold the _____ together c) to store _____ d) to soak up water and _____

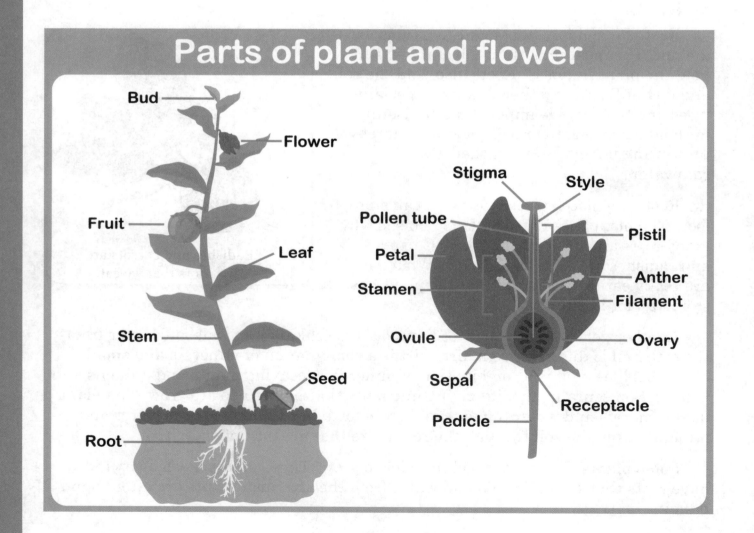

Parts of plant and flower

Bud

Flower

Fruit

Leaf

Stem

Seed

Root

Stigma

Style

Pollen tube

Pistil

Petal

Anther

Stamen

Filament

Ovule

Ovary

Sepal

Receptacle

Pedicle

B. Parts of a Flower

Plants reproduce in many ways. One of these ways is by making seeds. It is the job of flowers to make seeds, usually many seeds from one plant. Let us study the wonderful way that God enables flowers to make seeds.

 Practical Application: Study the parts of a flower.

Materials: a sweet pea flower, magnifying glass

Step 1: Using a magnifying glass, examine the petals of the plant. These petals, often colorful, attract insects to the blossom. Tiny leaf-like structures called sepals at the base of the petals protect the flower before it blossoms.

Step 2: Gently pull the petals away from the center and you will see the organs inside. Examine the exposed organs with the magnifying glass. You will see a collar-like formation of stamens; these are the parts of the flower that give rise to male cells. Each stamen has a structure at its tip called an anther that provides the pollen.

Step 3: Remove the collar of stamens to expose the pistil of the flower. The base of the pistil is called the ovary. If you split the ovary apart with your fingernail and examine it with the magnifying glass, you see will see the tiny ovules that may become seeds and grow into green peas.

Almost every plant in the world has flowers. Some are easy to see, like those on a rose plant. Some are much harder to see, like those of a maple tree. You must look very carefully.

The part of a flower that is the easiest to see is the petal. The petals are often festively colored and can be rather large.

The parts of a flower that surround the petals are called sepals. They are usually green and look like leaves. They protect the young flower as it grows. You can see the sepals of a plant when you look at the buds of a plant. When the flowers are ready to bloom, the sepals curl back and the flower is revealed.

Inside the petals are the seed-making parts of the plant. Around the center of the flower are string-like parts called filaments. These filaments have a black knob on top of them called the anther. The anther

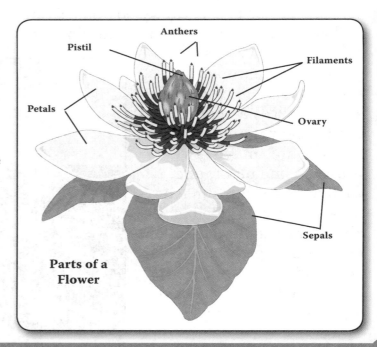

Parts of a Flower

is important because it makes pollen. The pollen is needed by the flower to make seeds. The filament and the anther make up the male part of a flower. The male part of a flower is called the stamen.

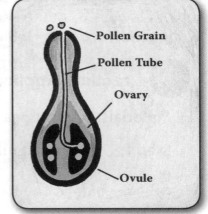

The female part of the flower is called the pistil. The top of the pistil is very sticky. The large part in the bottom of the pistil is called the ovary. Inside the ovary are tiny egg-shaped balls. These balls are called ovules. Most flowers have both stamens and pistils, as in a rose. In some plants, the male stamen is in one flower and the female pistil is in another flower, as in the case of a cucumber vine. Some flowers have only a stamen, others have only a pistil. The cucumber fruit grows from the flower that has the pistil.

Plants are essential for human life. In the Bible, in the book of Genesis, in Chapter 1, verses 11 and 12, we read what God created on the third day of Creation: *And He said: Let the earth bring forth the green herb, and such as may seed, and the fruit tree yielding fruit after its kind which may have seed in itself upon the earth, and it was so done. And the earth brought forth the green herb, and such as yielded seed according to its kind, and the tree that bears fruit, having seed each one according to its kind. And God saw that it was good.*

God made sure that there would be plenty of plants and trees for vegetables and fruit for all the people who would live on Earth. All the plants and trees would reproduce, and most of them would reproduce abundantly, that is, they normally would reproduce more than just once. They would multiply themselves over and over again.

Each year, millions of plants are used for food and building materials, yet most of the land on Earth continues to be covered with plants of all kinds! How can this be so? It is because God has given plants the ability to reproduce quickly and abundantly. This means that plants can produce many other plants like themselves. If you have a garden and plant a bean seed, you will find that one seed produces a single plant but the new plant contains many beans, maybe twenty beans on one plant, and each bean contains maybe 20 seeds! Just as God is abundantly generous in His gifts in the spiritual life, He is abundantly generous in providing for our physical growth and health as well.

Review Exercise II. B.

1. It is the job of flowers to make _____.

2. The female part of the flower is called the _____.

3. The stamen is the _____ part of the flower.

4. Most flowers have both stamens and _____.

5. We can read in the Bible in the book of _____ about the creation of plants.

6. God created the plants and the trees on the _____ day of Creation.

7. To make sure there would be plenty of food for all the people on Earth, God made sure plants would have the ability to _____ quickly and abundantly.

C. How Flowers Make Seeds

When the pollen in a plant reaches the pistil of the same kind of plant, this process is known as pollination. Pollination is the process coming before the reproduction of the plant.

 Practical Application: Examine the structure of seeds.

Materials: fresh green peas, dried lima beans, magnifying glass, tumbler, tap water

Step 1: Soak the lima beans in water for a day.

Step 2: Remove the green peas from their pods.

Step 3: With your fingernail remove the tough outside covering of both kinds of seeds and separate the two halves of the seed.

Step 4: Observe that the seed has two parts: the cotyledons, which contain stored food for the baby plant; and the embryo, which is snuggled between the cotyledons, and which grows into a baby plant. The growing embryo lives on the food that is stored in the cotyledons until it has grown its first green leaves above the ground.

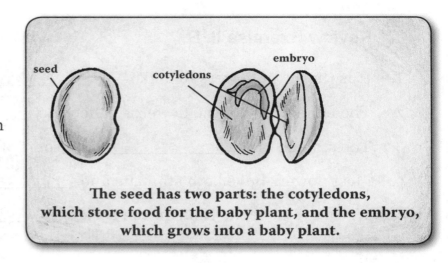

The seed has two parts: the cotyledons, which store food for the baby plant, and the embryo, which grows into a baby plant.

Pollination takes place in many ways. Sometimes pollen is carried from one plant to another by means of insects, such as bees. Insects are attracted by the bright colors and sweet smell of the flowers. The insects eat the sweet syrup called nectar, which is produced by the plants. As the insect feeds on the nectar, the insect touches an anther and pollen grains stick to the insect's body. When the insect flies to a flower of the same kind of plant, the insect leaves some of the pollen from the first plant on the sticky top of the pistil of the second plant.

Another way for pollination to occur is that instead of insects carrying the pollen, God arranged for birds or even the wind to carry the pollen from plant to plant. For a third way of pollination in some plants, God made the pollen simply drop from the anther to the pistil of the same plant! For a fourth way, some plants have an anther that "explodes," and sprays a small cloud of pollen into the air!

When pollen from the same kind of flower sticks to the top of the pistil, some of the pollen begins to form a tube down to the ovary. The pollen reaches the ovules in the ovary through this tube. The joining of male pollen grains with the female ovules is called fertilization. When fertilization takes place, baby plants start to grow in the ovules. Then the ovules begin to grow into seeds.

When the seeds are formed, the work of the flower is done. The flower then dies. New

Sepal

Immature, unreceptive stigma

Anther rubs against bee

Pollen grains stick to bee's abdomen

plants will grow from the seeds. In this way, usually one flower or plant reproduces in great quantity. If you plant one or two flowers of the same kind in your garden, you will find several more flowers the next year!

 Review Exercise II. C.

1. Pollination usually occurs when _____ carry pollen from flower to flower.

2. Pollination can occur when the _____ carries pollen to nearby flowers.

3. Sometimes pollen simply _____ from the anther to the pistil of the same flower.

4. Some plants simply explode and _____ pollen into the air.

5. The joining of male pollen grains with female ovules is called
    _____.

6. When the seeds of a plant are formed, the plant _____.

The way a flower dies in order to produce a
seed reminds us of how Jesus suffered and died
in order that we might have new life.

III. The Kingdom of Animals

A. Introduction

Like plants, animals are able to reproduce and grow. However, there are two basic ways that animals differ from plants. Animals can move and have senses.

1. Animals can move from place to place.

Generally, animals, such as cats and dogs, can move from place to place rather quickly and can even travel long distances. However, some "animals," like worms or shellfish, move rather slowly and not very far.

2. Animals have senses. They can see, they can smell, they can hear, they can touch, and they can feel if they are touched.

Animals also have knowledge, but theirs is only a picture type of knowledge, such as appears on a TV screen.

People have some things in common with the plants and animals. We can grow, reproduce, move from place to place, and have the sense of smell and touch and sight. However, we are superior to these other living creatures because God has given us an immortal soul with the ability to reason. With a human soul, God made us so we can think, come up with ideas, put ideas together to come to conclusions, and learn new ideas. Because of this great gift from God, we are able to know and understand things around us, we can think and speak to others, we can laugh at a joke, we can like and love other people. We can make things like a go-cart, or draw a picture.

In the Bible, God said *"Let us make man to Our image and likeness."* He meant that we have an eternal soul with reason which gives us the ability to think and with free will to love. Then God said, *"Let [man] have dominion over the fish of the sea and the fowls [birds] of the air, and the beasts [animals], and the whole Earth [plants and other things that grow], and every creeping creature that moves upon the Earth."*

Thus, in the very first book of the Bible, in Genesis, God gave people dominion or control over the whole Earth and every creature living upon Earth. Of course, God wants us to use the things of Earth for doing good for ourselves and for others, and for helping us live healthy lives.

Review Exercise III. A.

1. In what two ways do animals differ from plants?

   _____

   _____

2. What three things do we have in common with animals?

   _____

   _____

   _____

3. What immortal thing do we have that plants and animals don't have?

   _____

4. What are some things we can do that animals cannot do?

   _____

5. In the Bible, God said we should be in control of the _____ of the sea, _____ of the air, the beasts and things that grow, and every creeping creature.

B. Types of Animals

Biologists divide the animal kingdom into two basic types: the invertebrates and the vertebrates.

1. Invertebrates

Invertebrates are animals that do not have backbones. Such animals as sponges, jellyfish, worms, shellfish, and insects are common examples of invertebrates.

2. Vertebrates

Vertebrates are animals that have a backbone. Fish, frogs, turtles, birds, and cats are common examples of vertebrates.

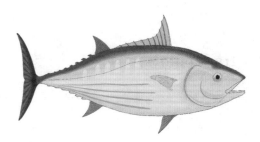

 Review Exercise III. B.

1. Animals that do not have backbones are called _____.

2. Fish, frogs, turtles, birds, and cats are examples of _____.

C. Insects

We can find insects almost everywhere on Earth. Because of their great numbers, they are the largest group in the animal kingdom. There are a number of reasons why more kinds of insects survive than all the other animals put together.

One reason is their small size. Therefore, they can live in tiny places where larger animals cannot live. Another reason there are so many insects is that they lay many, many eggs, thus producing many, many other insects. A third reason why there are so many insects is that insects can eat a great variety of food; they are always able to find food someplace.

A fourth reason there are so many insects is that many types of insects live in groups. This helps keep the survival of many members as they "help" each other to survive. Ants, bees, and termites are just a few examples of insects that live in groups.

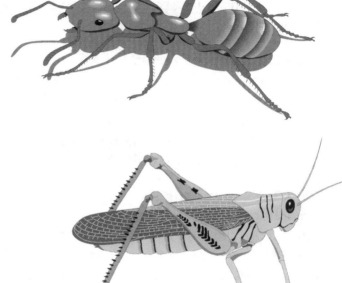

 Review Exercise III. C.

1. Insects can live in _____ places.

2. Insects lay many, many _____ and produce many, many insects.

3. Insects can eat a great _____ of food.

4. Many types of insects live in _____.

D. Characteristics of Insects

Biologists, scientists that study living things, say that an insect has three main characteristics: an outside skeleton, three body sections, and six legs.

 Practical Application: Study a typical insect - a grasshopper.

Materials: large jar, square of cheesecloth, rubber band, magnifying glass, a grasshopper (you can catch one easily in early summer in an empty field)

Step 1: Place the grasshopper in a large jar with fresh grass and twigs. Cover the jar with a piece of cheesecloth fastened with a rubber band.

Step 2: Examine the head of the grasshopper with your magnifying glass. Can you observe the eyes and the delicate antennae at the top of its head? Can you see the parts of its mouth at the bottom of its head?

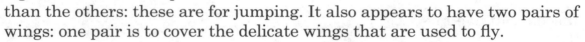

Step 3: Examine the thorax of the grasshopper with your magnifying glass. Can you see the three pairs of legs? Notice that one pair is thicker than the others: these are for jumping. It also appears to have two pairs of wings: one pair is to cover the delicate wings that are used to fly.

Step 4: The abdomen will have tiny openings in each of the segments that make up the back. The trachea is the network of tiny tubes throughout the body of the insect. These tubes connect to the outside through holes or openings. It is through these openings that the grasshopper breathes.

Step 5: After you have finished examining the grasshopper, release it so it can continue to live its life naturally.

1. An outside skeleton

A skeleton is the part of the body that holds it up and gives it shape. We have our skeleton of bones inside us. Insects have external skeletons.

2. Three body sections

These body sections are: the head, the thorax, and the abdomen.

The heads of most insects have antennae attached. These antennae help the insects sense the world around them. The eyes are on the head, as well as the mouth, through which the insects take in food by various means. There is a very wide variety in the shapes of the heads of insects.

The thorax is the middle portion of the insect's body. The legs of the insect are attached to the thorax.

The abdomen contains the parts of the body where food is digested and where the means of reproduction are located. The abdomen is attached to the thorax.

3. Six legs

An insect has six legs. They are attached to its thorax. If the insect has wings, then the wings are also attached to its thorax.

 Review Exercise III. D.

1. Biologists are scientists who study _____ things.

2. A _____ is the part of the body that holds it up and gives it shape.

3. The head, thorax, and _____ are the three body sections of an insect.

4. The legs of an insect are usually attached to the _____.

5. An insect has _____ legs.

6. If an insect has _____, these are attached to the thorax.

E. Metamorphosis

Metamorphosis means to undergo a change in physical appearance, in form, or structure.

Insects are tiny types of animals. Like all animals, they grow into adults. However, insects grow in a way that is different from most animals. As insects grow from egg to adult, they change form several times. Such dramatic changes in form in insects is called a metamorphosis (*meh-tah-morf-oh-sis*). *Meta* means change; *morphosis* means form. Other animals change as they grow, but they do not change form as much as insects.

Many insects change as many as four times before they become adults. Moths and butterflies are examples of insects that grow in this way. Biologists who study living things say that insects with four changes grow by a complete metamorphosis.

There are four stages of change or metamorphosis in insects.

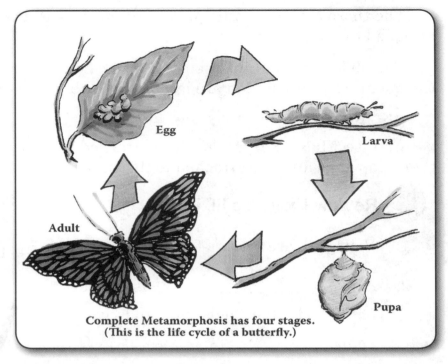

Complete Metamorphosis has four stages.
(This is the life cycle of a butterfly.)

1. In the first stage these insects are eggs. The eggs are laid by an adult female insect.

2. In the second stage, the eggs hatch. The insect is called a larva [plural is larvae]. Most people call them caterpillars. The larvae eat almost all the time. They eventually grow too big for their skins. The skins break apart and the larvae discard the skins. Some larvae discard four or five skins before they grow into the third stage of their life.

3. In the third stage, the larva finally stops eating and moving around. The larva builds a hard protective shell around itself. It has grown into a pupa. Inside this shell, the pupa grows into adult form.

4. In the fourth stage, after a period of time, the pupa shell splits open and the adult insect emerges.

Some insects go through three stages of growth. Grasshoppers and cockroaches are insects that grow in only three stages. Biologists say that these insects grow by incomplete metamorphosis.

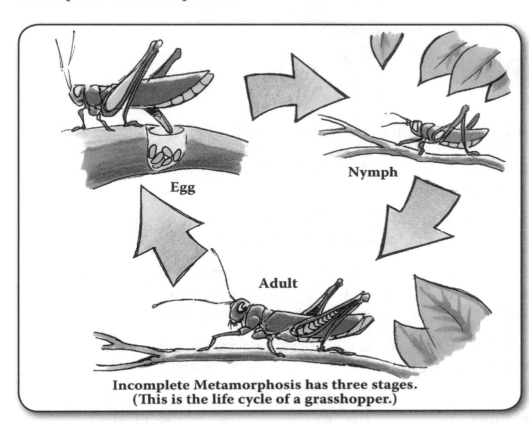

Incomplete Metamorphosis has three stages.
(This is the life cycle of a grasshopper.)

1. In the first stage these insects are eggs. The eggs are laid by an adult female insect.

2. In the second stage, the eggs hatch. The insect is called a nymph. The nymphs eat and grow. They also shed their skins as they outgrow them.

3. In the third stage, the nymph grows to the adult stage.

Review Exercise III. E.

1. Insects change _____ times by a complete metamorphosis.

2. In the first stage, insects are _____.

3. In the second stage, eggs hatch and are called _____ or caterpillars.

4. In the third stage, the insect lives in a shell and is called a

   _____.

5. In the fourth stage, the _____ breaks open and the adult

   emerges.

6. What is an example of an insect that grows by incomplete metamorphosis?

   _____

IV. The Kingdom of the Protists

Some living things are not clearly plants or animals. Because of this, biologists established a separate group called Protists. Examples of protists are algae and amoeba. We can study protists under a microscope.

A. Introduction

 Practical Application: Make a water-drop microscope.

Materials: aluminum foil, a 12" square of plastic, glue, medium size nail, small mirror, pencil, water

Step 1: Cut five or six strips of aluminum foil and paste them together with glue. Flatten them out by laying books on top of them.

Step 2: Punch a hole through the center of the aluminum with the medium size nail and smooth the ragged edges. Using a ruler to provide a straight edge, bend the strip of aluminum into the arch shape as shown.

Step 3: Place the aluminum strip on the square of plastic supported above the small mirror that reflects light upwards. Dip the pencil into water and place a drop in the hole.

Step 4: Place something underneath the "water lens" that you want to examine such as a hair or drop of water. Press on the plastic beside the aluminum arch to focus the "microscope."

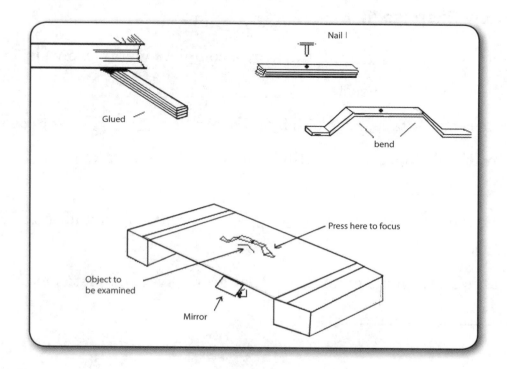

B. Members of the Protist Kingdom

 Practical Application: Observe members of protist kingdom.

Materials: a glass jar, some straw, pond water or water from a fish tank, microscope, an eyedropper

Step 1: Place the straw in the glass jar. Half fill the jar with pond water.

Step 2: Let the jar stand for five days in a warm place.

Step 3: After this time, put a drop of the water on a microscope slide and observe it under the microscope.

Notice: You should observe these very tiny one-celled organisms belonging to the protist kingdom. In particular, you should see paramecia and microscopic algae.

Many of the members of the protist kingdom are so small that one must use a microscope in order to see them. However, some, like algae, are much larger.

Some members of the protist kingdom are more like plants than animals. The algae, which contain chlorophyll and make their own food, are a good example.

Other members of the protist kingdom are more like animals than plants. The paramecium, which must hunt for its food, is a good example. The paramecium is a slipper-shaped cell that moves by means of short hairs called cilia. The cilia cause a current in the water in which it lives. This current carries food particles into a mouth-like hole or groove.

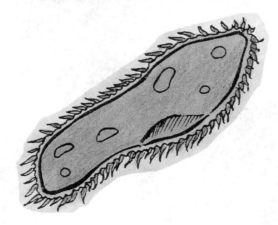

The paramecium is a slipper-shaped cell that moves by means of short hairs called cilia. The cilia beat back and forth like oars to make the cells move. The cilia also cause a current that carries food particles into a mouth-like oral groove.

Review Exercise IV. B.

1. _____ are more like plants than animals.

2. Algae contain chlorophyll like plants and thus make their own _____.

3. A paramecium is more like an _____ than a plant.

4. A paramecium must _____ for its food.

Green algae on rocks at ShihTiPing (giant stone steps) coastal area in Taiwan
by Fred Hsu

V. Bacteria

Bacteria are very, very small organisms. God created them so small that they can be seen only under a special microscope. Scientists say that millions of bacteria could fit on the head of a pin!

Bacteria are considered the simplest of all living things God has made. Bacteria are composed of exactly one small cell! These tiny bacteria cells come in three different shapes: round like a ball, oblong like a hot-dog, or twist-shaped like a spiral staircase.

Bacteria live all around us, as well as inside us, as well as in the plants, the ground, and animals.

Scientists who study bacteria have said that some bacteria are good and some are bad. Good bacteria help us digest our food in our stomachs. Bacteria live in animals also to help them digest their food. Bacteria help plants digest "food" from the soil.

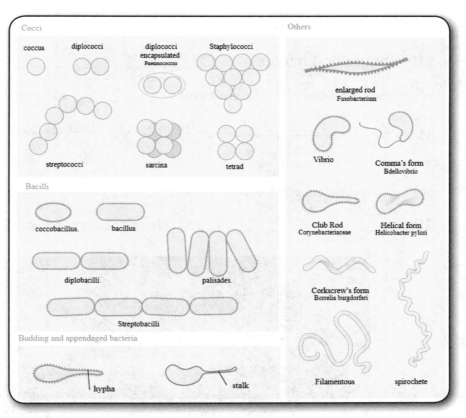

Bacteria Chart by Mariana Ruiz

Bad bacteria, called germs, collect on our hands when we touch dirty things. That is why we need to wash our hands frequently, and not put our fingers in our mouths.

Some bacteria can cause diseases. Normally our bodies can fight off diseases. When they cannot, scientists have discovered cures for most bacterial diseases. For instance, if you step on a rusty nail, the doctor will give you a tetanus shot to fight against the bacteria.

A strange thing about bacteria is that they help to produce yogurt and cheese in a process called fermentation! Fermentation is a chemical change caused by good bacteria.

Review Exercise V

1. Bacteria can be seen under a _____.

2. Bacteria are composed of exactly one small _____.

3. Good bacteria help us _____ our food.

4. Bad bacteria are called _____.

5. We must not put our fingers in our _____.

6. Some bad bacteria cause _____.

7. Scientists have discovered _____ for most bacterial diseases.

8. A _____ shot is given by doctors to those who step on a rusty nail.

9. Good bacteria help to produce yogurt and _____.

10. _____ is a chemical change caused by good bacteria.

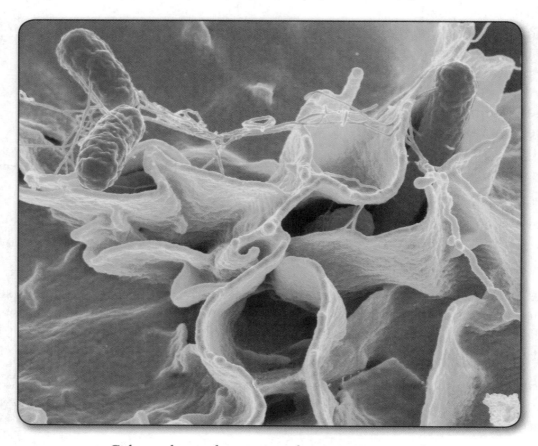

Color-enhanced scanning electron micrograph
showing Salmonella typhimurium (red) invading cultured human cells

Review for Chapter Six

Living Things

True or False -Please mark "T" for true or "F" for false.

_____ 1. Living things can move by themselves.

_____ 2. A biologist studies rocks.

_____ 3. Plants store food in their roots.

_____ 4. An insect is a vertebrate.

_____ 5. Protists are not clearly plants nor animals.

Please match the words on the left with the letter of their definitions.

_____ 6. angels   a. are pure spirits.

_____ 7. an insect   b. spins itself a cocoon.

_____ 8. a flower   c. has an outside skeleton.

_____ 9. the moth caterpillar   d. have immortal souls.

_____ 10. humans   e. is where seeds are made.

Please complete the sentences.

11. God makes all living things able to make new ones like _____.

12. A _____ is not clearly a plant or _____.

13. A plant has four major parts: flowers, _____, stems and roots.

14. Fish, frogs, turtles, birds, and cats are common examples of _____.

15. An insect undergoes _____ as it changes from egg to adult.

Circle the Correct Answer

16. The stages of complete metamorphosis are
      a) egg, larva, pupa, adult.   b) larva, pupa, adult, egg.
      c) egg, pupa, adult, larva.   d) pupa, larva, egg, adult.

17. What is not the name of a kingdom of living things?
      a) butterflies   b) plants   c) animals   d) insects

18. What is not a member of the Plant Kingdom?
      a) tree   b) radish   c) butterfly   d) cactus

19. What is not a member of the Animal Kingdom?
      a) a horse   b) a fish   c) a frog   d) a paramecium

20. What is not a section of an insect's body?
      a) head   b) thorax   c) abdomen   d) skeleton

"God created man in His Own Image...; male and female He created them."

Genesis 1:27

Introduction

In the Prologue of the Catechism of the Catholic Church, there is a statement about "The Life of Man." This is what the Church teaches.

God is infinitely perfect and holy. "In a plan of sheer goodness, He freely created Man to make him share in His own blessed life." Thus we see that God made people specifically to share in His goodness and in a holy blessed life in heaven so that we can carry out the vocation to which God calls us.

The Church teaches that God does not simply stand by and watch people from afar. He actually guides and inspires people. "...at every time and in every place, God draws close to man. He calls man to seek Him, to know Him, to love Him with all his strength."

God established a Church, the Catholic Church, by His Son Jesus. He established the Church to help people to understand more about Him, and to make it easier to be holy so as to attain eternal life in heaven. Thus, "He calls together all men... into the unity of His family, the Church. To accomplish this, ... God sent His Son as Redeemer and Savior. In His Son and through His Son, God invites men to become... His adopted children and thus heirs of His blessed life."

Gregor Mendel

Gregor Mendel was a priest and a biologist, that is, he was interested in studying living things. As a biologist, he was interested specifically in studying genetics, which is the study of genes. Genes are certain tiny cells inside all living things which contain instructions like a code on how living things grow and develop. These genes determine what a living thing will look like, how it will survive, and how it will interact with its environment.

It is the genes that contain the code for passing on characteristics from parent to offspring of living things. We call this heredity. Heredity is passed on through genes. When a child looks like one of his parents, we say that he inherited his good looks from his mom or dad. A child inherits the color of his hair and his eyes, the shape of his nose, and any of many other features.

Gregor Mendel

Gregor Mendel, being a good priest, certainly was helped in his studies of genetics by God and by the saints to discover the truth about heredity. Mendel's work was extremely important because it laid the foundation for modern scientists to study genetics.

Gregor Mendel was born in 1822 in a small village in Czechoslovakia. Mendel joined the Augustinian order of priests in 1843 and was ordained to the priesthood in 1847. He was assigned as a "supply" teacher in the local high schools. He was an excellent teacher and inspired great interest in natural science.

In 1856, he began a series of experiments on the common pea to determine the laws that govern the passing-on of characteristics from parents to offspring. He studied peas to discover which characteristics of a pea were passed down from the seed of a pea to the peas growing on the plant which developed from the seed pea. It is on this work that his fame in the scientific field rests. He is regarded as the founder of the science of genetics. Genetics is the science that studies genes and God's laws regarding heredity.

Gregor Mendel died in the monastery of St. Thomas in Brunn, Czechoslovakia, in 1884.

 Review Exercise

1. Mendel was a _____ and a biologist.

2. Mendel is the _____ of the science of genetics.

3. Genetics is the science that studies God's laws governing the passing-on of characteristics from _____ to offspring.

4. Genetics is the science that studies God's laws regarding _____.

Forget-me-nots
that demonstrate Mendel's rules

Outline of Chapter Seven

I. The Miracle of the Human Body
    A. How We Differ from Animals
    B. Cells: the Building Blocks of the Body
II. Bones
    A. Introduction
    B. The Skeleton
    C. The Protecting Bones
    D. The Spinal Column: the Backbone
    E. Caring for the Bones
III. Skin
    A. Introduction
    B. Skin Layers
    C. Caring for the Skin
IV. Growth
    A. Introduction
    B. Nutrition
    C. Food and Nutrients
    D. Healthy Eating

Chapter Aims

1. know how humans differ from other animals
2. know about the function of our skin and how to care for it
3. know about the function of our bones and how to care for them
4. know about the four food groups and what we need to eat to stay healthy

Activities

1. Look at onion cells
2. See the makeup of bones
3. See how your skin cools
4. Make a food chart

I. The Miracle of the Human Body

Of all of God's creations, the human being, made up of a physical body and a spiritual soul, is the most magnificent and complex creation. The human body makes up the material nature of man. God made the human body so it can grow and repair itself when damaged.

A. How We Differ from Animals

God has made humankind to be so much greater than any animals. God has given man intelligence, which includes the ability to reason and to learn. Most importantly, God has created man with an immortal soul, which contains an intellect and a free will. Because of our soul, we are able to do the following:

- know ourselves and other things the way they are;

- laugh;

- make things; and

- become sons and daughters of God for all eternity.

Every time we receive Jesus in Holy Communion, we become living tabernacles, holding Jesus inside of us. Because our bodies are "temples" of God, we must take good care of our bodies, and respect other peoples' bodies, so they are worthy of His Divine Presence.

 Review Exercise I. A.

1. The human body can grow and _____ itself when damaged.

2. Human intelligence includes the ability to reason and to _____.

3. Because we have an intellect and free will, we are able to know _____; to _____; to make _____; and to be sons and daughters of _____.

B. Cells: the Building Blocks of the Body

Cells are the smallest living units of our bodies and of every living organism. Cells are the basic building blocks of our bodies and of all living things.

Our bodies have many different kinds of cells. Each type of cell has its own special function or job to do in order to keep the body working. If we had only one kind of cell in our body, then we would not be able to do the wonderful things we can do. We have bone cells, skin cells, nerve cells, and many other kinds of cells which perform different functions. A group of the same kind of cells is called a tissue.

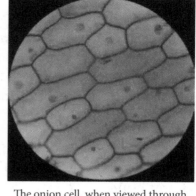

The onion cell, when viewed through the microscope, seems to be made of little boxes. Each of these boxes is a cell. A little piece of onion as big as this 'O' is made up of thousands of cells.

 Practical Application: Look at onion cells.

Materials: onion, knife, microscope, water, iodine, and eye-dropper

Step 1: Cut a slice of onion.

Step 2: Separate the layers.

Step 3: Find a thin sheet on the onion, like tissue paper, attached to each thicker layer. Remove one of these sheets from the onion.

Step 4: Put a drop of water on a microscope slide and add a touch of iodine to it. Put the onion sheet over the drop. The iodine in the water makes the cells easier to see.

Step 5: Look at the onion sheet under your microscope.

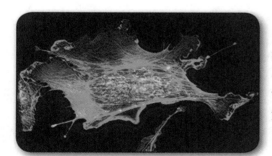

Cells are the smallest living building blocks of our bodies.

The different cells of the body all work together to keep our bodies healthy. Cells remind us of the different members of the Catholic Church who all work together to do God's work. As St. Paul writes in one of his letters:

"For the body is not one part, but many... You are the body of Christ, part for part."

1 Cor. 12: 14 & 27

Review Exercise I. B.

1. _____ are the building blocks of our bodies.

2. A group of the same kind of cells is called a _____.

3. The different cells of the body all work _____ to keep our bodies healthy.

II. Bones

A. Introduction

Our bones provide the structure for our bodies. Bones hold us in an upright position. Bones protect many of our internal organs.

The bones in our bodies come in all different shapes and sizes. Some bones are long, like those in the legs. Some bones are short, like those in the fingers. Other bones are round, like those in the neck. Some bones are flat, like those in the chest. Some bones, such as the skull, have a special shape all of their own.

A substance called marrow is inside the large flat bones of the body. The marrow is the place where blood cells are made. Marrow is the "blood factory" of the body, so healthy marrow is very important for our overall health.

We have over two hundred bones in our bodies. Each bone is made up of living cells and non-living materials. The non-living material is mostly calcium. Calcium is a mineral that makes bones strong. The non-living material weighs about twice as much as the living cells.

 Practical Application: See the makeup of bones.

Materials: chicken leg bone, glass jar with lid, vinegar

Step 1: Put the chicken bone in the glass jar.

Step 2: Fill the jar with enough vinegar to cover the bone.

Step 3: Wait a week.

Step 4: Remove the bone from the jar. Observe how it looks. Try to bend the bone.

The non-living mineral part of the chicken bone will have dissolved in the vinegar. The material that was once the living part remains.

 Review Exercise II. A.

1. Bones protect many of our _____ organs.

2. Bones are made up of what mineral? _____

3. Where is marrow found? _____

4. Marrow is the _____ factory of the body.

B. The Skeleton

God designed the bones in our bodies to form a skeleton. The skeleton is the framework of the body.

Our skeleton is important for the following reasons:

- The skeleton gives the body its shape, just like the framework of a building.

- The skeleton protects various special parts of the body. For example, the brain is protected by a special bone called the skull. Ribs are special bones that protect the heart and lungs.

- The skeleton helps us move parts of our bodies. The skeleton is like an anchor for the muscles and tendons. Muscles and tendons are the parts that we use in order to move our arms and legs.

- The skeleton is more marvelous than the framework of a building. The human skeleton is light, strong, and flexible. Moreover, unlike any frame made of wood, iron, or concrete, the human skeleton does not decay. The human skeleton is more unique than any frame that man can make because the human skeleton grows and repairs itself. God is very generous to have made us in this special way!

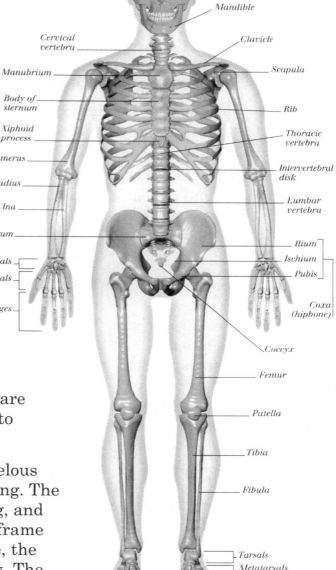

BONES OF THE BODY
There are four basic types of bones that make up the body's internal framework: long bones, such as the femur and humerus; flat bones, such as the ribs and most skull bones; short bones, such as the carpals and tarsals; and irregular bones, such as the vertebrae.

Skull

Mandible

Cervical vertebra

Clavicle

Scapula

Manubrium

Sternum — Body of sternum

Rib

Xiphoid process

Thoracic vertebra

Humerus

Intervertebral disk

Radius

Ulna

Lumbar vertebra

Sacrum

Ilium

Carpals

Ischium

Metacarpals

Pubis

Phalanges

Coxa (hipbone)

Coccyx

Femur

Patella

Tibia

Fibula

Tarsals

Metatarsals

Phalanges

Review Exercise II. B.

1. The skeleton is the _____ of the body.

2. Our skeleton is important because it gives the body its _____.

3. Our skeleton _____ various special parts of our bodies like our heart and lungs.

4. The brain is protected by a special bone called the _____.

5. The skeleton is like an anchor for the _____ and tendons.

6. Our skeleton is more wonderful than any frame that man can make because it grows and _____ itself.

C. The Protecting Bones

The brain is protected by special bones called the skull. The heart and lungs are protected by special bones called the ribs. These are the main protecting parts of the skeleton.

The skull is formed from eight cranial and fourteen facial skeleton bones. God has designed these bones to fit perfectly together, so as to form a protective shell or helmet for the delicate brain. The skull bone is about a quarter of an inch thick. The skull is thickest at the front and the back, where one is most likely to be hit. It is thin at the sides. Nerves run from the brain down to the spinal cord in the backbone. Thus, God made the bones of the skull with a hole at the bottom so the nerves can pass through the skull.

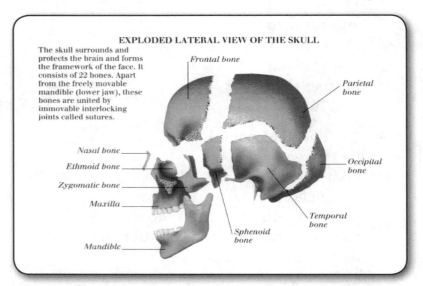

EXPLODED LATERAL VIEW OF THE SKULL

The skull surrounds and protects the brain and forms the framework of the face. It consists of 22 bones. Apart from the freely movable mandible (lower jaw), these bones are united by immovable interlocking joints called sutures.

Frontal bone
Parietal bone
Nasal bone
Ethmoid bone
Zygomatic bone
Maxilla
Occipital bone
Temporal bone
Sphenoid bone
Mandible

God has designed the ribs to protect the lungs and heart. Our ribs are long, curved bones that are attached to the breastbone in front and to the backbone or spinal column. Twenty-four ribs are arranged in twelve pairs. The ribs can move a little. When they move, they are pulled upwards and drawn outwards. This is the movement they undergo when we breathe. When we pull air into our lungs, we unconsciously pull our ribs upwards and outwards. When we push air out of our lungs, we unconsciously push the ribs back into their normal position. Try taking a deep breath while holding your hands on your ribs. Can you feel your ribs move?

Review Exercise II. C.

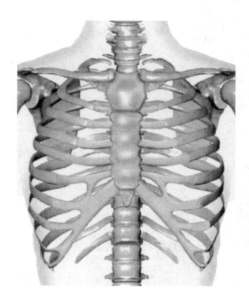

1. The heart and lungs are protected by the

   _____.

2. What does the skull protect?

   _____

3. The skull is formed from _____ bones.

4. What passes through the hole in the bottom

   of the skull?_____

5. What do the ribs protect?

   _____

6. What makes the ribs move up and out? _____

D. The Spinal Column: the Backbone

The most important part of the skeletal frame is the spinal column, often called the spine or backbone. The spinal column is so made that it holds up the frame of the body. The spinal column is very strong and flexible, and is made up of 33 little bones called vertebrae. The top seven vertebrae are in the neck. The next twelve vertebrae are behind the chest. The next five vertebrae are in the small of the back, while the last nine (sacrum and coccyx) are at the bottom of the backbone where the backbone joins to the hips. The vertebrae of the Sacrum and Coccyx are fused vertebrae.

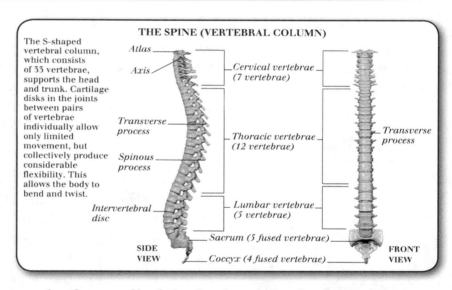

The S-shaped vertebral column, which consists of 33 vertebrae, supports the head and trunk. Cartilage disks in the joints between pairs of vertebrae individually allow only limited movement, but collectively produce considerable flexibility. This allows the body to bend and twist.

THE SPINE (VERTEBRAL COLUMN)

Atlas
Axis
Cervical vertebrae (7 vertebrae)
Transverse process
Thoracic vertebrae (12 vertebrae)
Transverse process
Spinous process
Lumbar vertebrae (5 vertebrae)
Intervertebral disc
Sacrum (5 fused vertebrae)
SIDE VIEW
Coccyx (4 fused vertebrae)
FRONT VIEW

In addition to supporting the skeleton of the body, the spinal column has another very important function. The spinal column protects the nerves that carry messages to and from the brain to the various other parts of the body. Inside the spinal column is the spinal cord which is a thick cable of nerves inside the backbone. The spinal cord passes through holes of each vertebra, just as the cord on our rosary passes through the holes in the beads. The little vertebrae that make up the spinal column protect the nerves, a very delicate but extremely important part of the body.

Review Exercise II. D.

1. The spinal column or backbone _____ up the frame of the body.

2. The backbone protects the _____.

3. Nerves carry _____ to and from the brain.

4. Each bone in the backbone is called a _____.

5. How many vertebrae are in the backbone? _____

6. The spinal cord goes through a hole at the back of each _____.

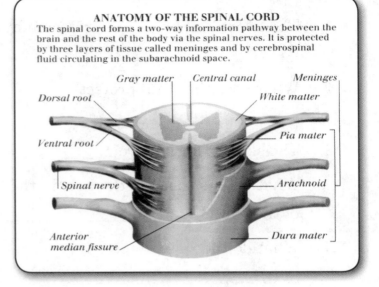

ANATOMY OF THE SPINAL CORD
The spinal cord forms a two-way information pathway between the brain and the rest of the body via the spinal nerves. It is protected by three layers of tissue called meninges and by cerebrospinal fluid circulating in the subarachnoid space.

Gray matter   *Central canal*   *Meninges*
Dorsal root   *White matter*
Ventral root   *Pia mater*
Spinal nerve   *Arachnoid*
Anterior median fissure   *Dura mater*

E. Caring for the Bones

Our ability to stand upright, to walk, to run, and to move depends greatly on the strength of our bones and the muscles needed to move our bones. Therefore,

we need to make sure that we care for our bones and muscles the way God intended. We care for our bones by making sure that the foods we eat contain the substances needed to build strong bones and muscles.

Some of the most important vitamins and minerals that strengthen our bones and muscles are calcium, phosphorus, Vitamin A, and Vitamin D. Vitamin D helps our bodies absorb and use calcium. These vitamins and minerals are contained in many different kinds of foods. The main foods are dairy products, such as milk. These vitamins and minerals are contained also in green leafy vegetables, fish, meat, chicken and turkey, eggs, whole grain breads and cereals, beans, and nuts.

Vitamin D is very important for the health of our bones and muscles. Vitamin D is known as the sunshine vitamin because our skin makes this vitamin from sunshine.

To keep our bones and muscles strong as well as healthy, we need plenty of daily exercise, especially outdoor exercise.

We can keep our bones and muscles healthy by eating wisely and playing outdoors, especially on sunny days.

We can help our bones grow straight by making sure we stand up straight and sit up straight, no slumping in a chair! By sitting and standing straight, we can help our bones grow straight. Standing and sitting straight relaxes our muscles and thus makes standing and sitting less tiring. If the back is straight, the rest of the body is in the correct position for strong and healthy bones and muscles.

Another way to take care of bones is to avoid accidents. A broken bone is painful and it keeps a person from doing things, such as playing games or going places, for several weeks. We should be careful about taking care of our bodies, especially since we want to be in good health for many, many years.

 Review Exercise II. E.

1. Name a dairy product we should drink every day for healthy bones. _____

2. Which vitamin helps our body to use calcium? _____

3. What makes Vitamin D through our skin? _____

4. How can we help our bones grow straight?_____

5. What should we be careful to avoid? _____

6. To keep bones and muscles strong, we need plenty of daily _____.

III. Skin

A. Introduction

The largest and most sensitive organ of the human body is the skin. Our skin covers and protects all the muscles, bones, and organs inside our bodies. When we think of our skin, we think of the sense of touch. Our skin helps us to learn about the things around us. That is because our skin has nerve endings that respond to touch and temperature. We rub our skin when we feel cold! Our skin keeps our bodies from losing water and drying out! Our skin guards our bodies against germs by preventing them from entering the body! That is why we wash our hands so often!

Let's make a list of what God has designed for our skin to do for us.

- Skin keeps our bodies from losing water and drying out.
- Skin guards our bodies against germs by keeping them from entering the body.
- Skin helps keep the body at the proper temperature.
- Skin helps us find out about the world around us because it has nerve endings.

Review Exercise III. A.

1. What is the largest organ of the human body? _____

2. What three things does our skin protect? _____

3. Skin keeps our bodies from losing _____.

4. What does our skin guard us against? _____

5. Skin keeps the body at a proper _____.

6. Skin helps us learn about the things around us with the sense of

   _____.

B. Skin Layers

The skin forms the outer covering of the body. The skin is made up of two layers: the epidermis and dermis. Each layer serves a different purpose in protecting the body.

The outer layer of the skin is called the epidermis. The cells in the epidermis are tough and flat. This layer of the skin protects our bodies from germs. This outer layer of skin also keeps our bodies from losing water.

Skin cells are constantly being made in the lower part of the epidermis. The new cells push the older skin cells to the surface. As the old skin cells come to the surface, they die. So the top part of the epidermis is made up of dead cells. The dead cells constantly chip off to make room for new ones. Your finger nails and toenails are thickened and hardened epidermis. You feel no pain when you cut them because they are made of dead cells.

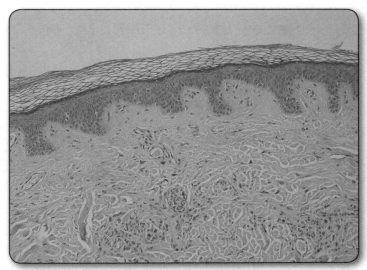

Example of normal epidermis and dermis tissue as seen through a 10x microscope

Below the epidermis is a much thicker layer of cells called the dermis. The lower layer of the dermis makes the skin flexible and tough. In the dermis are two kinds of glands: oil glands and sweat glands. The dermis also contains blood vessels, nerve endings, and hair roots.

The oil and sweat glands in the dermis produce oil and water. They pump oil and water out onto the skin. The oil keeps the skin soft. The water and dissolved salts given off by the sweat glands travel out onto the surface of the skin through little openings in the skin called pores. The sweat helps keep the body cool as it evaporates from the skin's surface, especially in very hot weather.

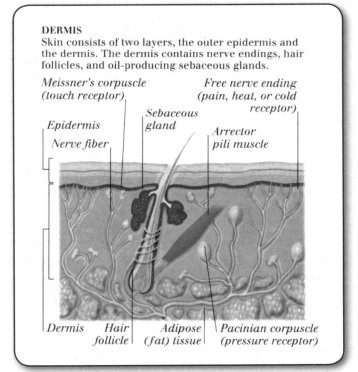

DERMIS
Skin consists of two layers, the outer epidermis and the dermis. The dermis contains nerve endings, hair follicles, and oil-producing sebaceous glands.

Meissner's corpuscle (touch receptor)

Free nerve ending (pain, heat, or cold receptor)

Epidermis

Nerve fiber

Sebaceous gland

Arrector pili muscle

Dermis *Hair follicle* *Adipose (fat) tissue* *Pacinian corpuscle (pressure receptor)*

★ **Practical Application**: See how the skin cools.

Materials: bowl of warm water and an electric fan

Step 1: Dip one hand into the bowl of warm water. Shake loose the water.

Step 2: Hold both your hands in front of the fan until they are dry. Which hand feels cooler?

Note: *When water evaporates, it cools anything it is in contact with. This is why your hand felt cooler. This is why perspiration cools your body.*

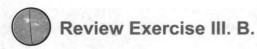

Review Exercise III. B.

1. Our skin has _____ layers.

2. The cells in the _____ are tough and flat.

3. The epidermis protects our body from _____.

4. The dermis makes the skin flexible and _____.

5. The dermis contains _____ _____, nerve endings, and hair roots.

6. The oil from the dermis keeps the skin _____.

7. The dermis contains _____ glands and _____ glands.

8. The water in the skin travels through little openings called _____.

9. The sweat keeps the body _____ as it evaporates.

C. Caring for the Skin

Since the skin is a very important part of the body, we need to make sure that we give our skin the proper care and attention. The skin provides a good reflection of the health of our inner body. We need to make sure that we eat the types of food that help our skin stay healthy and clear of problems.

To keep our skin healthy and smooth, it is important to eat the kind of good foods that make up a healthy diet in general. We should eat more yellow fruits and vegetables, as well as green leafy vegetables, like spinach, which are especially good for healthy skin.

Other foods which help to keep skin healthy are dairy products, especially milk, cheese, and yogurt. High protein foods good for the skin are fish, chicken, turkey, beans and nuts, seeds and whole grains, and eggs. Some fats and oils are important to keep the skin from becoming dry and flaky.

Although our skin needs the sunshine vitamin, Vitamin D, we must be careful not to expose our skin to too much sun, especially in the summertime. The sun's rays are strongest during the middle of the day so we need to be especially careful about not being in the sun too long at that time. Sunscreen creams can help to protect our skin from being burned.

We care for our skin by washing it regularly. Washing our skin helps to remove dirt, unpleasant body odors, and dead skin cells. Washing also helps to keep our pores and sweat glands open. Most important, washing keeps germs from entering the body.

Since cuts in the skin can allow germs to enter the body and even cause infections, we need to use soap and water to clean cuts. Even a small cut should be washed, and an antiseptic should be applied immediately, before the scratch, cut, or wound begins to close. Always tell your parents about any cut you may have so they can determine what needs to be done.

An important key for good health for our skin and body is prevention of accidents. Prevention of accidents is an important way to stay in good health. Accidents in the home are one of the most common and serious causes of poor health in children. Children can stay in good health and can prevent accidents by being smart and careful. For instance, don't stand on chairs. Don't leave toys and other items on the floor which might cause someone to fall. Keep hallways and stairs clear of clutter, such as clothes, toys, and boxes.

Videos are available free online for suggestions on how to prevent accidents in the home.

 Review Exercise III. C.

1. Which dairy products are good for healthy skin? _____

2. What color fruits and vegetables are good for the skin? _____

3. Which two high protein meats are good for the skin?

   _____

4. What are you likely to eat for breakfast that is good for the skin?

   _____

5. Washing helps to remove dead _____ cells.

6. Washing helps to open the _____.

7. A _____ cream can protect our skin from too much sunlight.

8. The sun's rays are at their hottest during the _____ part of the day.

9. Cuts in the skin can cause _____.

10. Prevent accidents by not standing on _____.

11. Prevent accidents by keeping steps and hallways clear of _____.

IV. Growth

We all know what we mean by the words "to grow." We know it means to change in size from tiny to bigger and to biggest. Did you ever stop to think about the amazing process of growing up? Have you ever thought about how it happens? How does a baby grow year by year? The answer is very complex.

When you were a little baby, your cells divided much faster than they do now that you are a young boy or girl. So your body grew strong enough to crawl, and then strong enough to walk, and finally, strong enough to run. God designed your body to have this special growing ability when He created you with the help of your mom and dad. As you become older, your growing ability slows down. As an adult, the only change that will occur to your body size will be to gain or lose weight. However, your cells will keep dividing as long as you live in order to replace damaged or worn-out cells.

A. Introduction

God has marvelously designed the human body with cells that "know" when to divide from one cell to two cells. Each cell divides to form two identical cells. The blood cells supply the other cells in the body with the energy that they need to divide. When a cell has enough stored energy to supply two cells, many changes begin to take place within it. When the changes have occurred, there will be two equal cells instead of one.

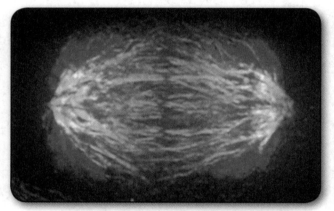

When the series of changes is complete, there are two cells instead of one.

When a skin cell divides, it forms another identical skin cell. A bone cell will form another identical bone cell. Sometimes one of the cells can die and be taken away by the blood as waste material. The body will not be damaged because the cell already has replaced itself.

 Review Exercise IV. A.

1. The human body has cells that divide from one cell to _____ cells.

2. Each cell divides to form two _____ cells.

3. The blood cells supply the other cells with the _____ to divide.

4. Sometimes a cell will die and be taken away by the _____.

B. Nutrition

Nutrition is the branch of science that deals with food and how food works in the human body. It includes studying all the things that are in food, such as vitamins, minerals, proteins, carbohydrates, and fats.

To help us know what the best foods are for us to eat, there is a special group of scientists called nutritionists who study nutrients. Nutrients are the substances found in food that give our body the energy it needs in order to grow and function.

Review Exercise IV. B.

1. The branch of science that deals with food and how it works in your body is called _____.

2. To help us know what the best foods are for us to eat, there is a special group of scientists called _____.

3. A _____ is a substance found in food that gives our body the _____ it needs in order to grow and function.

C. Food and Nutrients

It is important for us to learn about the foods that contain the kinds of nutrients our bodies need to stay healthy. God designed our bodies in such a way that they can automatically repair or replace worn or damaged cells with new strong cells. Bodies do this naturally and automatically; we do not need to think about doing this. However, we can help our bodies to grow strong and healthy by supplying them with the energy they need for cell replacement. We do this by eating the right kind of foods. Healthy food is the material that provides energy for our bodies to grow, develop, and stay healthy.

Review Exercise IV. C.

1. _____ designed the human body to grow, to develop, and to repair itself.

2. Our human bodies can _____ worn or damaged cells automatically.

3. Our bodies need _____ to do cell replacements.

4. _____ is the material that provides energy for the body to grow.

1. Vitamins:

Vitamins and minerals are important and essential nutrients our bodies need to perform different functions in our body. There are about thirteen known vitamins and minerals that are essential for the normal growth, activity, and repair of body tissues. A lack of certain vitamins can cause low energy and poor resistance to disease and illness.

Most foods we eat are rich in vitamins and minerals. Vitamins are produced in the cells of plants and animals. That is why it is important for us to include many different types of foods in our diets. Vitamin A, for example, is important in promoting good eyesight and helps the body to fight infection. The B vitamins help our cells use food for energy and keep our nerves and intestines healthy. Vitamin C increases resistance to infection. Vitamin D helps build strong bones and teeth. For other examples, see the Vitamin Chart.

Fruits, vegetables, beans and peas, dairy products, and meats are all excellent sources of vitamins and minerals. Whole grains, such as whole wheat bread, brown rice and oatmeal, are also rich in vitamins and minerals.

With help from your parents, you can learn to eat in a balanced way. Your parents know what foods are good for you to eat, and which are not.

Review Exercise IV. C. 1.

1. Vitamins and minerals are essential for the normal_____ , activity, and repair of body tissues.

2. A lack of _____ and _____ can cause low energy and poor resistance to disease and illness.

3. Vitamins are produced in the cells of _____ and _____.

4. It is important to include many different types of _____ in our diet.

The following vitamin chart is provided for reference only.

Vitamin	Uses	Source
Vitamin A (carotene)	Promotes good vision and healthy skin Important for growth and development Fights infection by strengthening the immune system	Deep yellow fruits and vegetables such as carrots, sweet potatoes, cantaloupe, apricots, leafy green vegetables, eggs, milk, cheese, and tuna

Vitamin	Uses	Source
Vitamin B1 (thiamine)	Promotes healthy nerve and muscle function Helps cells use food for energy	Whole grains, oatmeal, legumes, nuts, leafy green vegetables and some meats
Vitamin B2 (riboflavin)	Helps cells use oxygen Prevents skin disease and anemia	Milk, yogurt, eggs, cooked leafy vegetables, liver, broccoli, potatoes, poultry, fish, cottage cheese
Vitamin B3 (niacin)	Helps keep skin, nerves, blood cells and intestines healthy	Meats, poultry, fish, milk
Vitamin B6 (pyridoxine)	Improves mood and Helps with sleep disorders	Bananas, sunflower seeds, broccoli, avocados, brown rice, oatmeal, animal products, brewer's yeast
Vitamin B 12	Promotes normal growth, Promotes formation of red blood cells Maintains healthy nervous system and metabolism	Eggs, milk, yogurt, cheese, oysters, tuna, liver, and low fat animal products
Vitamin C (ascorbic acid)	Strengthens immune system Helps to heal wounds Reduces allergies and cold symptoms	Citrus fruits and juices, bell peppers, strawberries, papaya, broccoli, brussel sprouts and spinach
Vitamin D	Builds strong bones and teeth	Sunshine, milk, fortified dairy products, eggs, salmon and sardines
Vitamin E (antioxidant)	Good for immune system Helps to prevent cancer	Wheat germ, almonds, walnuts, leafy green vegetables, fish, chicken, turkey
Vitamin K	Bone health	Broccoli, leafy green vegetables, asparagus, cauliflower, lentils, chick peas and yogurt

2. Minerals

Just like vitamins, minerals are essential nutrients needed to help your body grow, develop and stay healthy, though only very small amounts are needed.

Some important minerals needed in small amounts are calcium, phosphorus, magnesium, sodium, and potassium. These are called macro minerals. Other minerals such as iron, iodine, and zinc are needed in still smaller amounts. These are called trace minerals.

Minerals perform many different functions. For example, calcium is an important mineral because it is needed to build strong bones and teeth. Calcium also helps muscles and nerves work quickly and smoothly. Calcium helps blood to clot when there is a cut in the body. Calcium is found in dairy products such as milk, cheese, yogurt, in dark green leafy vegetables, broccoli, and peas.

Potassium keeps your muscles and nervous system working properly. Many foods contain potassium. It is found in foods like bananas.

Magnesium helps the body utilize calcium and potassium. Magnesium is found in green vegetables, beans, peas, nuts, and whole grains.

Sodium is an important mineral but is needed only in very small quantities. We get enough of it in many of our foods and in table salt.

Iron is a mineral that helps red blood cells carry oxygen throughout the body. Raisins and spinach are high in iron as well as meats, turkey and fish.

Zinc helps your immune system and keeps your skin healthy. Zinc helps heal wounds such as cuts. It is found in high protein foods such as meats, dairy products, beans, and nuts.

Most minerals are found in the same kinds of foods in which we find vitamins, so children do not need to be concerned about getting enough of these minerals. A well balanced, nutritious diet will give you the necessary minerals and vitamins for a healthy body.

 Review Exercise IV. C. 2.

1. Some important minerals needed in small amounts are _____, _____, _____, _____, and _____.

2. These minerals are called _____ minerals.

3. Minerals needed in still smaller amounts are called _____ minerals.

4. _____ is an important mineral because it builds strong _____ and teeth.

5. _____ keeps our muscles and nervous system working properly.

6. _____ helps red blood cells carry oxygen throughout the body.

7. Most minerals are found in the same kinds of foods in which we find

_____.

The following Minerals Chart is for reference only.

Minerals and Their Function Chart

This chart is provided only to show how many minerals there are which God has made available for us to eat in various vegetables and fruits, and which are important for good health throughout our body systems.

Mineral	Uses
Calcium	builds bones & teeth, heart action, nerve impulses
Magnesium	bones, liver, muscles, transfer of intercellular water
Sodium	body fluid volume, nerve impulse condition
Potassium	cell membrane, nerve impulse conduction, heart rhythm
Copper	elastic tissue formation, cholesterol utilization
Zinc	protein synthesis, carbon dioxide transport, wound healing
Iron	hemoglobin formation, oxygen transport
Manganese	connective tissue, joint fluid production, nerve tissue
Chromium	insulin activity, heart muscle, cholesterol utilization
Phosphorus	builds bones and teeth, energy production
Silicon	bone formation, cartilage formation, elastic tissue
Boron	reduces calcium loss

Why are minerals important?

Minerals are required to put into action thousands of chemical reactions within the human body. Minerals can be obtained from vegetables and fruits.

3. Proteins

Proteins are very important nutrients that help your cells to grow and divide, and to build muscle and strength. Your muscles, your organs, and your immune system are made up mostly of protein. Protein builds up, maintains, and replaces the tissues in your body. Your body uses protein to make red blood cells that carry oxygen to every part of your body and helps to fight infections. Protein also helps the body digest foods, by making the digestive juices in your stomach and intestine go to work.

Many foods contain protein, but the best sources are beef, poultry (chicken and turkey), fish, eggs, all dairy products, nuts, seeds, and beans, especially black beans.

Review Exercise IV. C. 3.

1. _____ are nutrients that help our cells to grow and divide, and to build muscle and strength.

2. Made up mostly of protein are your _____, _____, and your _____ system.

4. Carbohydrates

Carbohydrates are nutrients that provide energy to the body and help the cells to carry out their specific tasks. Most importantly, carbohydrates are the major source of energy for the body.

There are simple and complex carbohydrates. Sugar is a simple carbohydrate, but it is not a nutritious one. It has no vitamins or minerals.

It's better to obtain your sugars from complex carbohydrates, foods like fruit and milk, because these contain vitamins, fiber, and important nutrients like calcium.

Some complex carbohydrate foods are better than others, such as whole grains (found in bread), oatmeal, rice, potatoes, raisins, fruits, beans and peas, corn, dates, apricots, nuts, honey, molasses, and dark green leafy vegetables. Complex carbohydrates are called starches.

Review Exercise IV. C. 4.

1. _____ are the major food source of providing the body with energy.

2. _____ carbohydrates are better than simple carbohydrates because they contain _____, _____, and important nutrients like _____.

3. Whole grains in bread are a good source of _____ carbohydrates.

5. Fats and Oils

When we talk about fats, it may sound like something to avoid, but that is not so. Fats and oils are nutrients that our body needs every day. Some nutrition experts say that calories from fat help the brain and nervous system develop correctly.

Fat is a component in many foods and an important part of a healthy diet. Some foods, like most fruits and vegetables, have no fat. Foods that do contain fat are nuts, oils, butter, and meats like beef. Salad oils, especially olive oil and fish oils, are excellent direct sources of the fats the body needs.

Fats help the body to burn food in order to produce energy. Fats and oils help in the process of building body tissue. Fats contribute to healthy skin, help fuel the body, help absorb vitamins, and provide the building blocks of hormones. Fats help people feel satisfied, so they don't eat as much.

 Review Exercise IV. C. 5.

1. Fats and _____ are an important part of a healthy diet.

2. Excellent sources of fats the body needs are _____ oil and fish oil.

3. The body needs _____ to burn food in order to produce energy.

4. _____ and _____ have no fat.

5. Children need fats and oils for proper _____ and nervous system development.

6. Water

All living things must have water to survive. Since about two-thirds of the human body is made up of water, we could not survive for more than a few days without water. Your body has many important jobs to do and it needs clean water to do them. For instance, water helps our bodies absorb digested food and water helps carry the digested food to all the cells in our bodies.

Water helps to remove body wastes and water helps fight off illness by carrying helpful cells more quickly to the part of the body which needs them.

Water is used by the body to cool itself in hot weather by sweating.

We could live about two weeks without food, but only a few days without water. Water is the key to our survival.

Water is found in fruits and vegetables, in milk and in other dairy products, in juices, in meats, and in other things we eat. There is no magic amount of water that children need to drink every day. It is important to drink when thirsty, and to drink more in warm or hot weather, especially when playing or exercising outdoors. Adults need more water than children.

When your body doesn't have enough water, we call that dehydration, which is a serious condition. You can tell you are dehydrated when you become tired, sluggish, or don't have as much energy as you'd like.

Dehydration can make you sick, so it is important to make sure you are drinking enough water or liquids that contain water, every day. For children, five glasses of water or juice a day can keep one healthy. Adults should drink up to eight glasses a day.

Pray for children in poor countries who cannot get enough clean water and often are sick.

 Review Exercise IV. C. 6.

1. People can live without water for only a _____ days.

2. About _____ of our body is made up of water.

3. When your body does not have enough water, we call that _____.

D. Healthy Eating

Throughout the years, nutritionists have designed food charts or pyramids recommending healthy eating practices. These were to serve as guides to what you should eat and the amounts you should be eating. The U.S. Department of Agriculture developed guidelines many years ago. These have been changed and modified through the years as new nutritional research was being done.

The most up to date recommendations have come from nutritionists at the Harvard School of Public Health, who found that the answer to good nutrition is actually pretty simple:

1. Eat a plant-based diet rich in fruits, vegetables, and whole grains.
2. Choose healthy fats, like olive and canola oil.
3. Limit red meat and unhealthy fats.
4. Drink water and other healthy beverages.
5. Limit sugary drinks and salt.
6. Exercise. It is a key partner to a healthy diet.

Practical Application: Choose MyPlate.gov

The illustration from the U.S. Government has been provided to help students realize the importance of eating a variety of food.

Fruits may be fresh or frozen or canned, or even dried fruit. 100% fruit juice is also excellent for good health.

Vegetables or 100% vegetable juice qualifies to fulfill the requirement. Vegetables may be fresh or frozen, raw or cooked, or canned. It is recommended that half your plate should be vegetables.

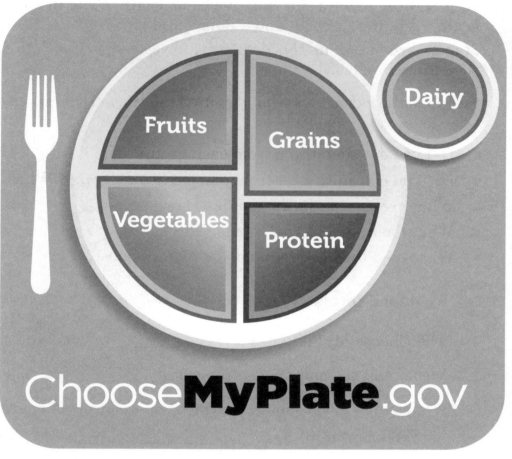

Whole grains or refined grains should be eaten every day during at least one meal a day. Encouraged are any food made from wheat, oats, barley, or rice. Foods containing these are cereals, oatmeal, bread, and pasta.

In the protein food group is included meat, chicken and turkey, seafood, beans, eggs, and nuts. In the dairy food group, milk and milk products which retain the calcium content are encouraged. Yogurt and cheese as well as puddings and other milk-based desserts are acceptable.

Eating healthy, taking time to walk, run, play, and exercise every single day, will keep your heart, muscles, and lungs strong and your body in condition. If you can walk or ride your bicycle instead of getting a car ride to wherever you are going, those activities can help keep you in good shape. And remember to get plenty of sunshine, the best source of Vitamin D to keep you well.

It is important to remember that God gave us wondrous bodies and that it is our responsibility to take care of them.

Practical Application: Make your own food plate.

Materials: pencil and paper

Step 1: Draw a plate showing five basic foods. Write in a fruit, vegetable, grain food, protein food, and a dairy product.

Step 2: Write down all the foods you ate yesterday. Check to see if you ate something in all food groups.

Step 3: Make a chart for what you ate yesterday. Then answer the following questions:

- Did you eat something from each group?
- Did you eat quite a bit from one particular group? Which one?
- What group of foods do you like the least?
- What foods should you start eating more?
- What food in each group do you like the most?

Review Exercise IV. D.

1. The Choose MyPlate is a _____ to what you should eat.

2. We should eat more foods from the _____ part of the plate.

3. A variety of foods should provide good amounts of energy from vegetables as well as protein, _____, _____ and _____.

4. A healthy natural beverage to drink is _____.

5. We should choose healthy _____ like beans or carrots.

6. Write two of your favorite fruits: _____, _____.

7. Physical exercise will keep your _____, your_____ and your lungs strong and your body in condition.

8. Plenty of _____ is a good source of Vitamin D.

Review for Chapter Seven

The Wonder of Man

Fill in the missing word or answer the question.

1. Gregor Mendel was a founder of the science of _____.

2. _____ are the smallest living units of the human body.

3. A group of the same kind of cells is called a _____.

4. A substance in the bones called _____ is where blood cells are made.

5. About how many bones are in the human body? _____

6. Which mineral makes bones strong? _____

7. The brain is protected by a special bone called the _____.

8. _____ are special bones that protect the heart and lungs.

9. How many ribs does the human body have? _____

10. The spinal chord/backbone protects a thick cable of _____.

11. Nerves carry _____ to and from the brain.

12. Each bone in the backbone is called a _____.

13. How many vertebrae are in the backbone? _____

14. Which dairy product should we drink every day for healthy bones? _____

15. What makes Vitamin D for our skin? _____

16. To keep bones and muscles strong, we need daily _____.

17. Skin keeps our bodies from losing _____.

18. Skin guards our bodies against _____.

19. Our skin has _____ endings that respond to touch.

20. The outer layer of skin is called the _____.

21. The lower layer of skin is called the _____.

22. The water in the skin travels through the little openings called _____.

23. Cuts in the skin can cause _____.

24. A _____ cream can protect skin from too much sunlight.

25. The human body has cells that divide from one cell to _____ cells.

26. The blood cells supply the other cells with the _____ to divide.

27. Human bodies can automatically _____ worn or damaged cells.

28. The science that deals with how food works in the human body is called _____.

29. The most important substance that human bodies need is _____.

30. _____ are produced in the cells of plants and animals.

31. Proteins help the human body fight _____.

32. Carbohydrates give the human body _____.

33. _____ are needed for strong bones and healthy teeth.

"May the God of peace Himself sanctify you in all things and may your whole spirit, and soul, and body, be preserved blameless for the coming of our Lord Jesus Christ."

1 Thessalonians 5:23

Introduction

Louis Pasteur was born in 1822 in Dole, France. He was one of the world's greatest scientists. He made major contributions to chemistry, medicine, and industry that have greatly benefited humanity. Louis Pasteur is remembered especially for his discoveries in the causes and preventions of diseases.

Louis Pasteur's discovery that diseases are spread by germs or bacteria has saved countless lives. In his work to kill germs, he discovered a method to preserve milk, beer, and other foods by which controlled heat is used to kill germs. This method is named after Pasteur; it is called **pasteurization**.

Pasteur proved that many diseases are caused by different types of germs that multiply in the body. His experiments proved that if these germs or microbes are weakened in a laboratory and then placed in an animal's body, the animal develops an immunity or resistance to the germ or microbe. He called this method of fighting off diseases vaccination.

Pasteur's Catholic faith was as strong as his interest in science. Some of his letters to his children were written with profound but simple piety. What he could not understand was the failure of some scientists to recognize the obvious evidence of the existence of God, our Creator, evidence that exists all around us in the world.

Louis Pasteur

Pasteur's son-in-law, who wrote the biography of Louis Pasteur, writes:

"Absolute faith in God and in Eternity, and a conviction that the power for good given to us in this world will be continued beyond it, were feelings which pervaded his (Pasteur's) whole life; the virtues of the Gospel had ever been present to him."

Louis Pasteur died in 1895, with a rosary in his hand, after listening to the reading of the life of Saint Vincent de Paul which he had asked to have read to him. Pasteur prayed that his own work, like that of Saint Vincent de Paul, would do much to save children from suffering from diseases.

Review Exercise

1. Louis Pasteur made major contributions to chemistry, _____, and industry.

2. Pasteur discovered _____, a method by which to preserve milk from germs.

3. Pasteur also discovered _____, a method to fight disease whereby an animal develops an immunity to a type of microbe.

4. Pasteur exhibited a profound but simple _____ in the practice of his faith.

5. Louis Pasteur prayed that his work would save children from _____ from diseases.

St. Luke Paints the Blessed Mother and the Child Jesus by Marten de Vos

Outline

I. **Personal Safety: Knowing Rules**
    A. Causes of Accidents
    B. First Aid

II. **Care of Nose, Throat, Ears, Eyes, Teeth**
    A. Nose: Avoiding Colds
    B. Throat: Treating a Sore Throat
    C. Ears: Protecting Your Hearing
    D. Eyes: Protecting Your Vision
    E. Teeth: Preserving Tooth Health

III. **Diseases**
    A. Deficiency Diseases
    B. Germ Diseases
    C. Bacterial Diseases
    D. Protozoan Diseases
    E. Viral Diseases
    F. Infectious Diseases

IV. **Immunity: Resistance to Illness**
    A. Your Body's Defenses: Immunity
    B. Staying Healthy
    C. The Family Doctor
    D. Wonder Drugs

St. Vincent de Paul

Chapter Aims

1. know the causes of the more common accidents
2. know the safety rules that will prevent accidents
3. know the things that are harmful to your nose, throat, ears
4. know the different ways to prevent harm to your nose, throat, ears
5. know the causes of disease
6. know major ways to prevent disease

Activities:

1. home safety rules
2. finding out about allergies
3. how pressure works
4. your resistance to diseases

I. Personal Safety: Knowing the Rules

Though your parents do their best to protect you and keep you safe, your personal safety is your responsibility and begins with you. To be responsible for your own safety, you must learn safe ways of doing things.

That is why it is important to know and follow rules of safety so that you can prevent accidents from happening. It is important to learn what to do in case they do happen. At all times, you must use your head and think before you act.

We cannot afford to be careless if we do not want accidents to happen. We have to take the extra time to learn the rules and to follow them, so that our actions safeguarding our safety will become automatic.

In this section, we will learn the causes of accidents and how to prevent them and what to do in case they should happen.

A. Causes of Accidents

Accidents can be caused by many things and by many different kinds of situations. We will learn about some of the most common causes of accidents.

1. Pointed Objects

Many accidents can and do happen when we play or work with pointed objects, such as pencils, pens, nails, knives, forks, scissors, or screwdrivers. Do you ever run or play with a pencil or pen in your hand or pocket? A pencil or a pen can be as dangerous as a knife! If a person falls while running or playing with any sharp object, he can be seriously injured.

Nails, too, can cause serious wounds if we step on them while barefoot or get scratched by them. Any wound can cause infection. If you see a nail or sharp object lying around in the garage, basement, or any place where a person may be walking, please pick it up and throw it away or put it in the right place where it won't cause anyone to be hurt.

All pointed objects should be handled with care. When handing a knife, screwdriver, or scissors to someone, do so with it pointed down toward the floor.

Here are four safety rules concerning pointed objects. Do you follow each one?

1. **NEVER** run while carrying a pointed object.
2. Carry a pointed object with the point down.
3. Tell your mom or dad if you see boards with nails or any other dangerous situation.
4. Hand a pointed object to another person with the point toward the floor.

2. Fire

Little kids often play with fire because they're curious and they don't understand how much damage fire can do. If you see a younger child playing with matches, candles, or any type of fire, get an adult right away!

Did you know that fire is the cause of many accidents? Even a very small fire can get out

www.fema.gov

Escape Plan

of control and burn down a whole house? Did did you know that many fires are started by children playing with matches or not being careful?

Fire moves very fast. A fire can burn down a building in minutes. And one burning house can set other houses on fire.

Fire accidents can be prevented if we follow rules of fire safety. A few easy steps can save a life. Here are a few fire safety rules to follow:

Rule 1. Have a smoke detector and a fire extinguisher.

Smoke detectors with a working smoke alarm and fire extinguishers should be in every home. A smoke detector sets off an alarm which goes off if smoke is detected. Be sure you know how to use a fire extinguisher. It is recommended that one is kept in the kitchen.

Rule 2. Be careful when cooking.

The U.S. Government reports that not paying attention or wandering off when cooking is the leading cause of home fires and fire injuries in the United States. We must be very careful when cooking and we must know what to do should there be a fire.

a. Grease fires: If a pan with grease catches fire, never throw water on it! It will spatter hot oil in addition to continuing to burn. Immediately grab a lid or large plate and slip it over the pan. The fire will go out, because a fire needs air to burn. Do not try to cover the fire from the top of the pan. Slip the cover from the side of the pan, so your hand and arm are away from the fire. Children should immediately yell for parents or older people to help.

b. Microwave fires: When cooking in a microwave, do not use metal objects or aluminum foil, since they could start a fire. If a fire starts in a microwave, keep the door closed. It will go out if the door is closed.

Rule 3. Be careful with matches.

We must be very careful using matches to start a fire, or when we are around any kind of fire, such as outdoor cookouts, fireplaces, or bonfires. Do not help with starting a fire without asking permission from an adult. Many children are hurt each year due to being unaware of the danger of fire.

Rule 4. Be careful around open flames.

Many fires are caused when people brush their clothes against open flames. Always be careful near any kind of flames and do not stand, sit, or walk too close to any flames.

Should your clothes ever catch on fire, grab a blanket or towel and put it over your body. If this is not available, throw yourself down on the floor or ground and roll over the flame until it goes out. If you see someone else's clothes catch on fire, quickly cover him with a coat or blanket or anything nearby to smother the flames. If nothing like that is available, push the person to the ground and instruct him to roll over on top of the flames.

Rule 5. Practice a fire drill and escape plan.

Every family should practice a fire drill and have a plan in case of a fire. This should include wall charts of exit routes from each room in the house.

Some families have a specially designed roll out window ladder they keep on the second floor. Other families keep thick ropes near a window or under a bed. If none of these are available and you need to get out a window, a rolled-up sheet can take the place of a rope or ladder. A sheet can be rolled into a rope, then tied or attached to a heavy bed or piece of furniture in the room and put out the window to climb down on.

Rule 6. Post fire safety rules.

Fire departments have free posters with Rules for Fire Safety. Perhaps you can ask your mom or dad to take you to the fire department to get one, and to post it in the kitchen for all to see. Fire safety information and videos for children are available on the Internet.

 Review Exercise I. A. 1.

1. We should never _____ while carrying a pointed object.

2. When handing knives or screwdrivers to someone, we should hand the object with the point _____.

3. The leading cause of fires in the home happen in the _____.

4. The quickest and safest way to put out a grease fire in a pan is to

_____.

5. If anyone's clothes catch fire, the best way to put the fire out is to throw a

_____ or _____ over it to smother the flames.

3. Medicine

Medicines often save lives. When a doctor prescribes a medicine to anyone, it is meant to help that person get well and to stay well. Medicines are only for the person to whom it is prescribed. Though it is good for that one person, it can act like a poison for another person. No one should take anyone else's medicine. Sometimes, even for the person for whom it is prescribed, if too much of certain medicines is taken, it can make that person very sick.

Accidents with medicines can happen. Nurses in hospitals must read and re-read the labels on medicines when they give medicine to the patient, so as not to make a mistake. In this way, they are doubly sure that patients, especially children, are safe.

Children should not ever take any medicine without their parents giving it to them. Parents will read the label and the directions and make sure children are taking the right amount at the right times.

Rule: Children should never take any medicine by themselves. Never, never, never!

4. High Places

Most boys and girls your age like to climb. Climbing can be fun and safe if you follow these few safety rules:

1. Climb only on things built for climbing, such as a ladder or the climbing bars on the playground.
2. Hold on with both hands. Do not be a show-off.
3. Wear shoes with soft soles rather than shoes with hard, slippery soles.
4. Never climb near a window or glass door.
5. Ask your Dad to get a ladder when he puts up curtains or changes a light bulb. Falling accidents happen to children and adults, and often result in a broken bone.

5. Electrical Appliances

Electrical appliances are wonderful inventions! They serve many good purposes in the home and help make daily life easier and more comfortable. However, electrical appliances can be dangerous if not used properly or handled properly. Any time we handle any electrical appliances, we need to remember safety rules. Thousands of children are hurt each year because of accidents with electrical appliances.

A main reason that children get hurt is because they become used to seeing their parents using electric appliances, so children are not aware of the dangers.

All electrical appliances, when plugged into an outlet, must be kept away from water. We must never touch any electrical appliance with wet hands. If you touch a radio, for instance, with wet hands, you can get an electrical shock. Sometimes families have a radio in the bathroom, which can be dangerous because of the use of water in the bathroom. As a rule, radios should be kept out of the bathroom.

A worn cord on a plugged in electrical appliance can expose the bare wire. A bare wire can give a person a shock, or even cause a fire. The local fire department can tell you how many fires in your community have started because of electrical or wiring problems. Either replace a worn wire or throw the whole appliance out.

Rules to Remember:

- Never turn on a light switch or electrical appliance while you are wet.
- Never leave electrical cords where people might step on them or trip on them.
- Never touch electrical outlets with your fingers or with objects.
- Ask your mom or dad to help you change light bulbs.
- In case of an electrical fire, get out of the house immediately!
- Never use water to try to put out an electrical fire; you could be killed.

 Practical Application: Talk to your parents about home safety rules:

1. Changing a light bulb

2. Using a toaster

3. Using kitchen appliances, such as a mixer or microwave

4. Using a computer or printer

5. Machines or appliances not to be used except by parents

 Review Exercise I. A. 2.

1. Medicines are only for the person to whom it is _____ by a doctor.

2. A medicine can be good for one person, and act like a _____ for another person.

3. When needing to reach a high place, climb only on things designed for climbing, such as a _____ and make sure you keep your balance.

4. All electrical appliances must be kept away from _____ and not touched with wet _____.

5. A bare or stripped wire can give a person a shock, or even cause a _____.

6. Swimming

Swimming, especially on very hot days during the summer, is a very enjoyable activity and exercise. However, as with anything, you must know the rules in order to enjoy this sport safely. For people between the ages of 5 and 24, drowning is the second leading cause of accidental death and injury. Hundreds of children die each year from swimming accidents. If you follow a few simple rules, you can enjoy this activity safely.

Rule 1: Know how to swim. If you do not know how to swim, ask your parents to give you swimming lessons or take lessons at places like the YMCA or 4-H Club.

Rule 2: Once you learn how to swim, never, ever, go into a swimming pool without an adult or lifeguard being present to supervise and to watch you in the pool. Never!

Rule 3: Never swim alone. Swimming is a sport that needs a buddy system. Always swim with a partner, every time, whether you're swimming in a backyard pool or in a lake. Even adult and experienced swimmers can get muscle cramps or become tired out, which might make it difficult to get out of the water. When you swim with a "buddy," he can help or go for help in case of an emergency.

Rule 4: Most swimming pools have a shallow and a deep end. Unless you can swim very well, stay in the shallow water so that your feet can touch the bottom of the pool.

Rule 5: Avoid rough play. Be careful and avoid rough play with others. Dunking and splashing others may seem like fun, but this kind of play in the water can be the cause of serious accidents.

Rule 6: Keep a floating device nearby. It is important to have a flotation device or a "life-saver" in or near the water in case you or your buddy encounter a problem staying afloat. Keeping these safety rules in mind will make your swimming experience a pleasant and safe one.

7. Wheel Sports

Bicycles, roller blades, and skateboards are fun to ride and can be a great opportunity for healthy exercise, games, and enjoyment. But it is important to remember that these are not toys but moving objects on wheels, like vehicles. Because they take on great momentum or speed with you on them, they can be a cause of serious accidents as well, especially if you should fall.

A good part of staying safe in wheel sports depends on how well you can handle them and stay safe. Take the time to learn these sports well and to follow the safety rules. Then you are less likely to have accidents on wheels. There are a number of safety rules you should know and practice each time you get on a bicycle, on roller blades, or on a skateboard.

Rules for bicycle safety:

1. Inspect your bike and make adjustments.
2. Wear a helmet.
3. Always stay on the right side of the bicycle path.
4. Look out for hazards or obstacles which might cause an accident.
5. Obey stop signs.
6. Know and use hand signals when you want to make a turn.
7. Keep a horn, a light, and a reflector on your bicycle.
8. Stop and wait when someone is in your way.

Skating safety rules:

1. Take skating lessons.
2. Wear a helmet. It's the law in most states.
3. Wear kneepads, elbow pads, and wrist guards.
4. Use your head: don't take risks!
5. Never skate in the street. Look for a designated skateboarding area.
6. Don't be a show off! Some people spend weeks or more in a hospital because they thought it was "cool" to respond to a dare or to show off.
7. If you lose your balance, crouch down so you don't need to fall so far.
8. If you start to fall, try to roll rather than absorb the fall with your arms.

Just as a reminder: About 30,000 people a year are treated for skateboarding injuries. Six out of ten injuries are to children under 15 years of age. One-third of the children injured have been skateboarding for only one week. Injuries are due to falls when the skateboard hits something irregular on the surface, or are due to riders attempting stunts. Riders should check the surface to have a better chance of not having accidents. Skate in a designated skateboarding area. Never skateboard in the street.

 Review Exercise I. A. 3.

1. To avoid swimming accidents, it is important to learn how to _____.

2. Swimming is a sport that needs a _____ system. This means that we should always swim with a _____.

3. Even the best swimmers can get _____ and need the help of other people.

4. One thing we should always wear when bicycling or skating is a

   _____.

5. Bicycles, roller blades, and skateboards are like _____ because they take on great speed.

Review Exercise

1. List two of four safety rules concerning pointed objects.

   _____

   _____

2. What should you do if the pan on the stove catches on fire?

   _____

3. Why can taking someone else's medicine be dangerous?

   _____

4. List three safety rules that make climbing ladders safe.

   _____

   _____

5. List three safety rules for using electrical appliances.

   _____

   _____

6. List four safety rules for swimming.

   _____

   _____

7. List five safety rules for riding a bicycle. _____

   _____   _____

   _____   _____

8. List three safety rules for skating.

_____

_____

_____

B. First Aid

First aid is an emergency medical treatment given to people who become sick or injured before professional medical care or an ambulance arrives on the scene.

The first thing to do in medical emergencies is to call 911 so that medical help can come as quickly as possible.

The best way to learn and know what to do for unexpected accidents before any help can arrive is to take a class in First Aid. The Red Cross, some hospitals, and some fire departments offer free First Aid classes. There are some free courses online. However, taking a Red Cross class, or one given by a fire station, gives a student practice in learning what to do in emergency situations and will keep one from being nervous or afraid. It is a good idea for everyone in the family to take a course in how to provide first aid.

1. Helping accident victims

Do you remember the story told by Jesus about the Good Samaritan?

"A man fell victim to robbers …. They stripped and beat him and went off leaving him half dead …. A Samaritan traveler who came upon him was moved with compassion at the sight. He approached the victim, poured oil and wine over his wounds, and bandaged him. They he lifted him up on his own animal, took him to an inn and cared for him" (Luke 10).

Most boys and girls your age are not old enough or know enough to treat those who are sick or injured. However, you are old enough to call the emergency number 911, the police, a doctor, or other adult for help. However, you may do things that the sick or injured person asks for or that will help to make the person more comfortable.

You are really growing up when you can provide some help for an injured person. Many hospitals and fire stations offer free First Aid classes to children. It is especially recommended for teens who are baby sitters.

Let us pray that we, too, would respond to victims of accidents by getting help from adults and by giving whatever first aid we would be capable of giving.

Listed below are the ways we can help others who need our help:

a. Calling 911 on the telephone. Medical help would arrive almost immediately.

When we see that someone has been hurt or has been in an accident and there is no one else around to help, it is best to call the number 911 on the telephone and report the accident immediately. You will need to give your name, your location, and a description of what has happened. The operator at 911 will help you to know what you can do and will send an ambulance or policeman to provide whatever kind of help is needed.

b. Treating a Bruise

The most frequent injury many of us experience is a bruise. A bruise is an injury that is caused by a hard blow to our body, or a fall that does not break the skin but makes the skin change color.

The best way to quickly treat a bruise is to put something cold on it, such as an ice pack or any frozen bag of food from the freezer. However, most doctors recommend a thin cloth be placed between the ice pack and the skin so as not to hurt the skin. Most people keep at least one ice pack in their freezer for such occasions. The application of an ice pack causes the blood vessels to become smaller in the bruise. Then it doesn't swell as much as if it were warm. You might need to apply the ice pack for a few minutes, never longer than 10 minutes at a time, take it off for a few minutes, then reapply it again for a few minutes.

If you do not have an ice pack, pour very cold water on the bruise, or if possible, soak the bruised part in a pan of cold water. You could wet a towel or wash cloth in very cold water, and apply it to the bruise. When the towel or cloth warms up, be sure to replace it with another cold one.

 Review Exercise I. B. 1.

1. First aid is an _____ medical treatment to someone who is sick or injured.

2. The first thing to do when we see someone who is sick or injured is to call _____.

3. The best way to treat a bruise is to put something _____ on it.

c. First Aid for Burns

Burns to any part of the body fall into three categories, depending on how serious they are. These are called first, second, and third degree burns. Most common household burns are scalds from extremely hot water or liquids, steam, and cooking oil that splatters. These types of burns fall into the small burns category, or first degree burns, and can usually be treated at home.

More serious burns, burns of the second and third degree, require medical care or hospitalization. Hospitals are able to handle all kinds of burns and to stop any infections that can result from burns to the skin and body.

The best first aid for any burn is to cool the burned part of the body as quickly as possible by plunging the burned part into ordinary cool water (not cold or icy) to reduce the temperature of the area and to reduce any further damage to the skin. This will help to relieve the pain and to stop the burning.

For small burns, aloe vera gel can be applied. Various burn ointments or antibiotic creams can be used. These are available from the local drugstore or pharmacy. It is wise to keep some of these on hand in the house. These ointments stop the pain and keep the skin from blistering and becoming infected. A recent recommendation in a medical journal noted that plain honey helps to reduce the pain from a burn, keep it from blistering, and keeps the area free from infection.

Children should report any and all burns to their parents because of the possibility of infection. Parents are in a position to decide whether further medical care is needed.

 Review Exercise I. B. 2.

1. The best first aid for any burn is to _____ the burn as quickly as possible with _____ water.

2. Most household burns can be treated at _____.

3. More serious burns require _____ care or hospitalization.

4. Small burns can be relieved by applying _____, _____, or _____ creams.

d. Treating a Cut

Cuts, scratches, and abrasions are a part of growing up. Cuts are injuries to the skin caused by something sharp, like a knife. Scratches are slight injuries that happen when a sharp object, like a thorn, piece of metal, or sharp fingernail scrapes your skin. Abrasions are scrapes on your skin that can happen when you fall on a sidewalk and scrape your knees. Each of these can cause your skin to bleed. The blood will usually clot and form a scab as it heals. A scab usually falls off within a week or two. Try not to pick at scabs as that can interrupt the healing process.

The best way to treat a small cut is to pour a capful of hydrogen peroxide (only the 3% kind) on the cut to kill any germs there. It will foam on the cut. (Be sure to do this with parental supervision and to put the top back on so none will spill from the bottle.) Then wash the wound with soap and water and clean the wound of any dirt. Soap and water alone will clean and kill the germs.

After the cut is cleaned, dab some iodine on it, and let it air dry. After this dries, place a germ-free (or sterile) bandage over the cut to protect it. The bandage should be replaced the next day, or if it becomes wet or dirty, replace it with a fresh one sooner. Some small cuts heal faster if exposed to the air.

Some cuts are serious and need to be looked at and treated immediately by a doctor. If the cut is deep, it may need stitches. Stop any bleeding first by pressing it with your hand. If you can, press a clean, soft cloth against the wound. If you don't have a clean cloth, use a pillow case or undershirt or skirt or anything clean that has a smooth surface. Hold your hand over the cloth and apply pressure until help arrives or until someone takes you to the doctor. Release every so often for a few seconds, then press again.

Always tell your parents of any cuts, scratches or abrasions you have. They will know what needs to be done.

 Review Exercise I. B. 3.

1. Cuts, scratches, and abrasions can cause your skin to _____.

2. The blood will usually clot and form a scab as it _____.

3. Picking at a scab can interrupt the _____ process.

4. Pouring hydrogen peroxide on a cut will kill any _____ there.

5. If the cut is deep, it may need _____.

6. Always tell your _____ of any cuts you have.

2. Family Safety

You may know the old saying, "An ounce of prevention is worth a pound of cure." The "ounce" represents the little bit of time, care, and attention that is required to stay safe, and to prevent an accident from happening. The "pound of cure" is the great amount of time, care, and attention that is required to devote to the treatment and recovery from an accident.

There are many small things in your family requiring small amounts of attention that should be practiced daily in order to maintain everyone's safety and prevent accidents from happening. When people live together, they all share in the responsibility of keeping each other safe in their home.

You may need to talk and work with your family so that everyone cooperates in creating a safe environment. How can this be done?

Here are a few things that you and your family can do:

1. Make sure there is no clutter on the stairs or in the hallways.
2. Pick toys up off the floor.
3. Keep kitchen utensils out of the reach of toddlers.
4. Keep sharp things out of the reach of babies.

When you say your daily prayers, pray for the safety of your family. Many saints are patrons of various physical problems. St. Herman the Cripple was born in 1013 in Germany with cerebral palsy. His parents did not know how to take care of him, but they realized that he was brilliant. They took him to be raised by monks in an abbey in southern Germany when he was only seven. He later became a Benedictine monk. The monks recognized him as a genius and allowed him freedom to study, to write, to discover. According to one report, "he studied and wrote on astronomy, theology, math, history, poetry, Arabic, Greek, and Latin. He built musical instruments, and astronomical equipment." He was considered "the most famous religious poet of his day" and is the author of the famous hymn Salve Regina. Pray to St. Herman for the safety of your family.

Review Exercise I. B.

1. The help given to someone who is sick or injured is called _____.

2. A _____ is an injury caused by a fall or a hard blow that does not break the skin but makes it change _____.

3. The best way to treat a bruise is to put something _____ on it.

4. The best first aid for any burn is to _____ the burned part of the body as quickly as possible.

5. If possible, plunge the burned body part into _____ in order to ease the pain and stop the burning.

6. The best way to treat a small cut is to pour _____ (only the 3% kind) on the cut to kill any germs there.

7. Something that is germ-free is said to be _____.

II. Care of Nose, Throat, Ears, Eyes, Teeth

A. Nose: Avoiding Colds

The first sign of a cold is a runny nose. Colds are usually caught from people who already have a cold, and who breathe, cough, or sneeze in the close presence of others. The germs that cause colds need a warm, moist place to live, so they are usually spread through the nose or mouth. You can "catch" a cold by being too close to someone who has a cold. When a person sneezes, coughs, or breathes in your face, the germs are passed on to you. Be very careful to stay away from someone with a cold as germs are very contagious.

Be sure you do not spread a cold. If you have a cold, be sure to cover your mouth and nose when you cough or sneeze. Many people cough or sneeze into their sleeve. Keep your hands away from your nose and use a tissue or handkerchief. Wash your hands after blowing your nose because you can spread germs with your hands when you touch anyone. If you can, stay away from other people so that they do not "catch" your germs. Remember, a thoughtful Christian person does his best to keep others from getting sick. In hospitals, nurses are often required to use a mask over the mouth and nose when they are around sick people.

It is also important to keep yourself clean. One thing germs are afraid of is soap and water. Wash your hands often, especially during the cold season. Wash your hands especially when you cough or sneeze or blow your nose, before touching or eating food, after playing outside, after visiting sick relatives or friends, after using the bathroom and after playing with pets and animals. And keep your fingers and such things as pencils out of your mouth that may have a lot of germs on them. Practicing good habits will help you keep from catching a cold.

A good way to avoid a cold is to keep your immunity strong. We do that by keeping ourselves as healthy as possible. To stay healthy, eat right, get the sleep you need, and get enough sunshine and exercise.

B. Throat: Treating a Sore Throat

St. Blaise is the patron saint for those with throat illnesses.

Our throat does not need any special attention until those times when we get a cold. A cold often leads to a sore throat. An old and simple remedy to soothe a sore throat is by gargling with warm salt water several times during the day. Your parents can show you how to do this and how much salt to put into a glass of warm water.

When you have a cold, drink plenty of liquids such as hot tea or broth. Hot chicken soup is good both for a cold and a sore throat. In addition to hot soup, it is also soothing on the throat to drink hot tea with honey. Even just hot water with honey and lemon soothes a sore throat. Parents sometimes buy flavored zinc lozenges that help heal a sore throat.

Review Exercise II. A. & B.

1. You can catch a cold by being too close to people who _____, _____, or breathe in your face.

2. One thing germs are afraid of is _____ and _____.

3. Frequent _____ of hands, especially during the cold season, can prevent colds.

4. A simple remedy to soothe a sore throat is by _____ with warm salt water.

5. When you have a cold, drink plenty of _____.

C. Ears: Protecting Your Hearing

1. Air Pressure

Have you ever had a strange feeling in your ears when coming down in an elevator or in an airplane? Swallowing several times will help you to get rid of this feeling. Why do you think swallowing affects your ears?

The strange feeling you sometimes get in your ears is caused by air pressure. If the air pressure is not the same on both sides of your eardrum, your ears feel blocked or tight. When you swallow, air is able to enter and leave your middle ear through a tube to your throat. Then the air pressure becomes the same on both sides of your eardrum.

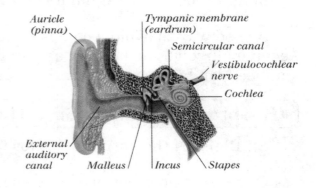

The tube connecting your middle ear to your throat is called the Eustachian (u stak' ki en) tube. By means of your Eustachian tube, air pressure is kept the same on both sides of your eardrum.

Practical Application: How Pressure Works.

Blow up a balloon. What happens if you continue to blow, making the air pressure on the inside of the balloon much greater than the air pressure on the outside?

2. Blows

A blow on the ear forces air against the eardrum very rapidly and may harm it. Do your best to protect your ears from any blows, especially when you are playing sports.

3. Infections

Do you know what an infection is? An infection is a disease caused by germs. If an infection develops in your middle ear, outward pressure may push against your eardrum. This pressure may cause your eardrum to bulge and become painful.

The first sign of an infection in the middle ear is often an earache. Whenever you have an earache, you should tell your parents immediately. Your parents may call a doctor. By getting proper medical care quickly, you may avoid a serious illness as well as any loss of hearing.

4. Loud Noises

Have you ever heard the high-pitched whine of a jet plane? Loud noises such as this may cause sound waves strong enough to harm your ears. Even listening to music that is too loud can hurt your ability to hear and can cause long-term damage. Doctors have found that young people are listening to very loud music and, as a result, more middle-aged people are showing signs of hearing loss. It is wise to open your mouth when you are going to hear a loud noise. Then some of the sound waves reach your ear through your Eustachian tube. There is then less danger of harming your eardrum because there is pressure on both sides of it.

5. Wax

The wax produced in the auditory canal of your ear stops dust and dirt from getting far into the ear. However, sometimes the glands that form wax make too much wax. Then the auditory canal becomes blocked, and you cannot hear well. Do not try to remove some of the wax yourself. Only a doctor, nurse, or other skilled person should remove the wax. Be sure to tell your mother or father if you have trouble hearing. Never put anything in your ears. Serious damage can result from a foreign object in the ear.

6. Water

Sometimes water enters the auditory canal of your ear when you are swimming. Although this water cannot get into your middle ear because it is blocked by the eardrum, the water may make you very uncomfortable. If you have had ear trouble in the past, be sure to check with your mother or father before going swimming. They may tell you not to swim underwater or not to dive into deep water.

Review Exercise II. C.

1. The strange feeling you sometimes get in your ears when coming down in an elevator or in an airplane is caused by _____ _____.

2. You can get rid of that strange feeling of tightness in your ear by _____ several times.

3. The tube connecting your middle ear to your throat is called the _____ _____.

4. A disease caused by germs is called an _____.

5. It is wise to open your _____ when you are going to hear a loud noise.

6. The _____ produced in the auditory canal of your ear stops dust and dirt from getting far into the ear.

7. Water in the auditory canal of your ear cannot get into your middle ear because it is blocked by the _____.

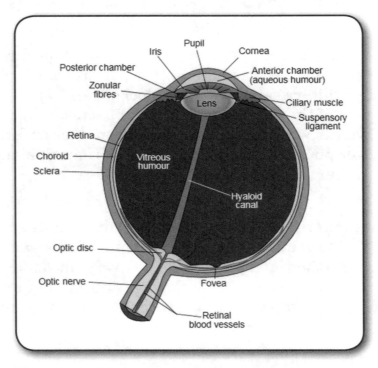

Diagram of the Human Eye

D. Eyes: Protecting Your Vision

We depend on our eyes in almost everything we do, from the moment we open them in the morning, to the time we close them as we fall asleep at night. We experience the world we live in primarily through our eyes. The eyes work together to help us see people and things around us and to judge how close or how far things are from us. Our eyes automatically adjust to sunlight and to darkness so we can find our way around.

Because our eyes and the gift of sight are so important, it is a good idea to have periodic eye exams with an eye doctor, called an optometrist or an ophthalmologist. We should remember to pray to St. Lucy, the patron saint of those who are having eye problems.

In young children, eye rubbing, tearing, or redness, and difficulty following an object with the eyes are signs of vision problems. Older children may squint or sit too close to the TV to be able to see more clearly. Things may be out of focus. Children who are having trouble seeing might complain of headaches at the end of the day because they have been straining their eyes during the day.

If you are having any of these problems, be sure to tell your parents so they can take you to an eye doctor to have your vision checked. The solution is usually as simple as getting a pair of eyeglasses. Eyeglasses can help you to see things that were hard to see clearly before. Your optometrist will have many styles of glasses for you to choose from.

We must protect our eyes by keeping them clean and free from dust and dirt. If any kind of speck gets into our eyes, our eyes will be irritated and begin to produce tears. However, we should never rub our eyes because rubbing can scratch the delicate tissue of the eye. If there is no help around, you can pull gently on the lashes of the upper lid and pull the lid down over the lower lid. Do this several times if necessary. Usually the speck of dirt will come out easily. For anything that will not come out easily, tell your mother or father as soon as you can. But do not rub your eye!

 Review Exercise II. D.

1. Our eyes automatically _____ to sunlight and darkness.

2. It is important to have regular eye exam with the _____doctor.

3. _____ can help you to see things that were hard to see clearly.

4. The _____ will have many styles of glasses for you to choose from.

E. Teeth: Preserving Tooth Health

In past times, people did not understand how to take care of their teeth. Because they did not know that it was important to keep their teeth clean, their teeth began to decay and would either fall out or need to be pulled out.

Today, we know what causes tooth decay, known as cavities, and other tooth and gum problems. Today, we have highly qualified dentists and dental assistants who examine our teeth regularly, about twice a year, clean them thoroughly, and if necessary, repair our teeth. They instruct us on how to care for our teeth daily so that we can keep them strong and healthy throughout our lives.

Why is it important to take care of our teeth? It is important to take care of our teeth because when we eat, bits of food particles are left between the teeth and gums. If we do not dislodge the particles, the bacteria already present in our mouth begin to multiply. These bacteria cause the formation of plaque, which eventually causes tooth decay and later, gum disease.

Recent studies are showing that the bacteria between the teeth and in the gums can show up as bleeding gums, cavities, or even swelling of the tongue and gum tissue. It can actually be the cause of other diseases later in life.

The following are some recommendations on how to keep teeth and gums in a healthy state:

1. **Banish bacteria.** Bacteria not only cause cavities, gum disease, and bad breath, they also produce acid, which then causes more tooth decay. Sugar is what bacteria feast on. Sugar causes tooth decay and gum disease to develop much faster. To get rid of harmful bacteria, remove plaque by flossing once a day, and brushing teeth at least twice a day.

2. **Reduce acid exposure.** Because sugar, sodas, and fruit juices can erode enamel and soften the tooth's protective covering, either rinse your mouth or brush your teeth after drinking them.

3. **Eat teeth friendly foods.** Crunchy raw apples, fresh carrots, and nuts can mechanically clean teeth as you chew them, so they make good desserts or snacks. Good bacteria present in yogurt can reduce the acidity and bad bacteria in your mouth and stomach.

4. **Brush your teeth correctly and gently.** Brush gently up and down for a minute or two. Follow with flossing or if possible, flush water between your teeth to remove food between the teeth.

If you take care of your teeth **daily** and visit your dentist regularly, twice a year, you should be able to keep your teeth healthy.

III. Diseases

A disease is like an illness or sickness that interrupts the normal functioning of our body. However, it is possible to have a disease and not be sick, and it is possible for a person to be sick and not have a disease.

Most diseases are caused by very tiny, microscopic organisms called germs. No one can promise that you will never be ill. Most people are ill at one time or another. However, most of us can get well on our own because God has provided our bodies with protections which can defeat most of the germs that can cause us to get sick.

When you say your nightly prayers, be sure to thank God for your good health. Pray, also, for the good health of the rest of your family.

In this section, we will learn about different diseases and their causes. What are germs? Where are they to be found? How are they carried from one person to another? How does your body fight them? What can you do to defend yourself against them? These are a few of the questions that will be answered in this section.

If you get sick, remember to offer up your sufferings for the souls in Purgatory. Our sufferings can be offered up in union with Jesus for the sinners of the world that they may return to Jesus with love.

A. Deficiency Diseases

There are diseases which result from a **lack** of a certain essential vitamins or minerals. These are called deficiency diseases. Our bodies stay healthy as long as we eat foods that provide vitamins and minerals.

Two well known deficiency diseases are scurvy (sker' vi) and rickets (rik' its). Scurvy is a deficiency disease caused by a lack of Vitamin C. Rickets is a deficiency disease caused by a lack of calcium, phosphorus, and Vitamin D.

Children who eat exclusively only three or four certain foods may suffer from deficiency diseases. In the United States, such deficiency diseases are rare because good food is easily available. However, if children do not eat what their parents give them to eat, such as fruits and vegetables, such children can suffer illnesses because of a lack of proper vitamins and minerals.

B. Germ Diseases

Do you catch a cold once or twice a year? Have you ever had to stay home because you had measles, mumps, or chicken pox? All these diseases are caused by germs.

The word *germ* is just a convenient way of referring to certain kinds of microbes (mi' krobz). A microbe is a very tiny living organism that is so small it can be seen only under a microscope. Disease germs are microbes that can cause us to get sick.

If germs get into your body, they can cause disease in two ways. Some germs destroy body cells. Other germs make poisons that keep parts of your body from working as they should. Either way, germs can make you very sick.

1. Germs Travel

Germs travel from one person or creature to another. For example, some diseases are carried by insects, such as flies, ticks, and mosquitoes. These diseases can be controlled by getting rid of the insects that carry them. For example, swamps can be drained, so that mosquitoes cannot lay their eggs there.

Larger animals can carry disease. People can contract diseases from rabbits, parrots, cats, deer, even dogs. At one time, many people fell ill with tuberculosis by drinking milk from cows that carried the disease. Today, cow's milk is made safe by pasteurization (pas cher e za' shen) in which the milk is heated to a high temperature in order to kill any possible germs. It is then chilled and sold.

2. Germs multiply

Germs are very tiny microscopic organisms. It would take about five thousand of the largest ones to make a line one inch long. Why are they so dangerous? They are dangerous because they increase so fast and move easily from person to person and can be the cause of a serious illness.

Many families use special cleaning agents to kill germs, bacteria, or viruses that may be on kitchen counters or in bathrooms or on doorknobs, telephones, and other places which many people touch with hands that may not be very clean. If these cleaning solutions are not available, regular soap and water can kill many germs.

Sometimes children don't realize that if silverware is not properly cleaned with very hot water, germs can pass around the family. While dishwashers may seem like a luxury, in a family with children, the very hot water and very hot dry air kills most if not all germs on plates, cups, and silverware. People should not drink out of each others cups or eat off of each others plates. That is inviting germs and illness.

 Practical Application: Examine a Drop of Water.

Boil some dead grass in a pan of water. Put the pan aside for a few days. Then look at it. Smell it. Is there scum on the water? If you have a microscope, use it to look at a drop of water containing some of the scum. What do you see? Do you see any living things in it?

Now boil some fresh water. Look at a drop of this water under your microscope. Are there living creatures in it? Report what you see.

C. Bacterial Diseases

Bacteria (bak tir'e a) are certain one-celled living organisms that tend to live in the human body. Most kinds of bacteria are not harmful. There are good bacteria and bad bacteria. In fact, we could not live without bacteria. Many good bacteria live in our bodies and are necessary for proper digestion.

Bacteria, however, are a type of germ. Bacteria multiply by dividing. When bacteria reach full size, they break into two. Some bacteria are fully grown within twenty minutes.

Where do we find bacteria? Bacteria are everywhere. They are in the air, in the human body, and on everything you touch. The bacteria to watch out for are the bad bacteria.

There are some kinds of bacteria that can make you very sick. If they get into a break in your skin, they can cause your skin to become infected. Some bacteria can even give you blood poisoning.

Bacteria can spoil food and make it dangerous to eat. That is why food should be put in the refrigerator right after a meal. Bacteria grow quickly in food that sits out in room temperature.

Bacteria can cause such diseases as diphtheria (dif thir'i e), tuberculosis (tu ber'kyu lo' sis), typhoid fever, and scarlet fever. Fortunately, we do not have these diseases in this country to any extent because Americans visit their doctor on a regular basis. It is important, however, to know how to defend your body against harmful kinds of bacteria.

D. Protozoan Diseases

Some germs are single-celled living organisms. They are called protozoans (pro te zo' enz). Most protozoans live in water. If you took a drop of pond water and looked at it under a microscope, you would probably see many protozoans. These very tiny organisms are helpful to man in some ways. However, a few kinds cause diseases. African sleeping sickness and malaria are both caused by protozoans. Fortunately, these diseases are not common in the United States.

E. Viral Diseases

A virus is a very, very tiny cell-like type of germ which multiplies after it invades a body cell. Viruses can do a great deal of harm within a very short time.

You have probably heard a great deal about viruses (vi' res ez). They cause such common diseases as influenza (which we usually call flu), mumps, measles, chicken pox, and polio. They also are responsible for colds and cold sores. Viruses can be seen only with the aid of the most powerful microscopes. Scientists have learned how to prevent and to treat certain virus diseases. Nevertheless, scientists believe that they still have much to learn about viruses.

F. Infectious Diseases

Diseases that can be carried from one person to another are called infectious (in fek' shes) diseases. Infectious diseases are also called communicable diseases because they can transfer from one person to another. How are infectious diseases spread? That depends on the disease.

The germs that cause colds, for example, can travel from one person to another with a cough or sneeze. The germs are carried into the air and breathed in with the air. That is why it is important to stay away from other people when you have a cold, as well as to stay away from people who have colds. What seems to be a cold may be the beginning of a more serious disease, such as the flu.

 Review Exercise III.

1. What is meant by a deficiency disease? _____

2. Define microbes. _____

3. Define bacteria. _____

4. Define protozoans. _____

5. What are the two ways by which germs can cause disease in your body?

    _____   _____

6. Where can you find bacteria? _____

7. Explain why not all bacteria are harmful? _____

    _____

8. Name several diseases caused by bacteria. _____

    _____

9. Name two diseases caused by protozoans. _____

10. Name several diseases caused by viruses. _____

    _____

11. How are diseases are carried from one person to another?

    _____

12. Why are germs dangerous? _____

13. What are infectious diseases? _____

    _____.

IV. Immunity: Resistance to Illness

Our body's defense system against illness and disease is called immunity. Our immune system is composed of cells, tissues, and organs that protect us against the invasion of germs which can cause disease. A person who is healthy and strong is said to have immunity or high resistance to disease and illness. This means that his or her body can usually fight off disease-causing germs. This person stays well most of the time and seldom must stay home because of illness.

A. Your Body's Defenses: Immunity

Our bodies have a number of very effective ways to keep us healthy by not allowing germs to enter or to multiply.

1. Skin: Keeping Germs Out

With so many germs all around us, you may wonder how you ever stay well. The reason is that your body has several good ways of defending you against germs. In the first place, your body is completely covered by protective skin. In addition, your body openings have a lining of mucous membrane. Most germs cannot pass through your skin nor the mucus membrane to get inside your body.

2. Mucous Membrane: The Germs You Breathe

Many germs are not able to enter your body. Since there are germs in the air, you breathe them in through your nose and throat. Do you know how your body resists many of these germs? Cilia in your nose and windpipe strain out dust and germs. Cilia are the tiny hairlike parts in the inner lining of the nose and windpipe.

In addition, your nose, throat, and windpipe are lined with a mucous membrane. Large numbers of germs are trapped in the sticky mucus. When you blow your nose, cough, or sneeze, you get rid of most of these trapped germs.

3. Hydrochloric Acid: The Germs You Swallow

You not only breathe in germs, but you also swallow them. They are on your food. They are on the hands that touch your food. If you put fingers or pencils into your mouth, you put germs into your mouth as well.

Some of these germs go down into your stomach. Many of them are killed in your stomach. Your stomach makes a strong acid that helps digest food. This acid, known as hydrochloric acid, kills many germs that might reach your stomach.

4. White Blood Cells

Some germs get through the body's outer defenses and somehow go into the blood. However, the blood has a way of fighting germs. If you look at a drop of blood under a microscope, you may see both red and white cells in it. The white cells are the blood's germ killers. They can rush to the germs, surround them, and destroy most of them.

5. Fever and Antibodies

The white cells do not always succeed in killing all the germs that enter your blood. Some may be carried to various parts of your body. Even then, however, God gave your body ways to defend itself. For one thing, you may develop a fever to attack the bacteria. Because some kinds of bacteria can live only at certain lower temperatures, when your body raises its temperature with a fever, these germs will die from the heat.

There is another way that your body fights germs. God designed your body so that it can form antibodies (an' ti bod eez) which are like little chemical weapons which are sent into your bloodstream. An antibody is a substance produced by the body that counteracts the effects of germs or poisons from the germs. There are different antibodies for different diseases. The antibodies stay in your blood even after you get well. They keep you from getting some diseases a second time. We say that the body is then immune to that disease.

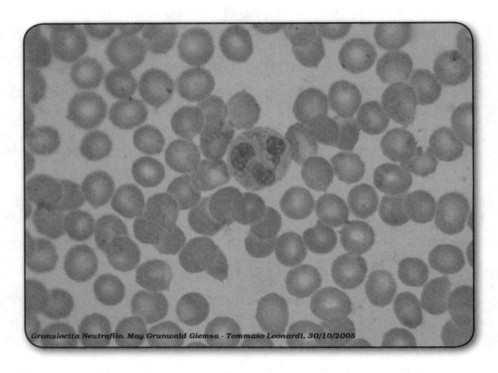

Granulocita Neutrofilo, May Grunwald Giemsa - Tommaso Leonardi, 30/10/2005

Neutrophil granulocytes are the most abundant type of white blood cells in mammals and form an essential part of the immune system.

Review Exercise IV. A.

1. What are two "first lines of defense" that your body has for keeping germs out?

   _____

2. How do your nose and throat defend themselves against germs you breathe in?

   _____

3. How does your stomach defend itself against many germs?

   _____

4. How does the blood fight germs? _____

   _____

5. How is a fever a way the body defends itself against germs?

   _____

6. Define antibodies. How are they different from other ways the body fights

   disease? _____

   _____

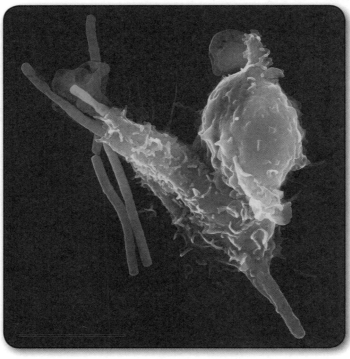

Neutrophil engulfing anthrax bacteria
by Volker Brinkmann

B. Staying Healthy

It is no fun to be ill. In fact, you feel miserable and you miss doing many things you enjoy. How can you stay well? How can you help your body to stay healthy and to resist illness and disease? If you practice good health habits every day, you can count on staying well.

Good health habits mean getting enough rest and sleep. Many children fight going to bed. They wear out their parents as they continually get out of bed, go to get a drink of water, play with their toys, and find endless excuses for not staying in bed. Not getting enough sleep lessens the body's ability to fight off diseases and germs.

Good health habits include plenty of outside play in the sunshine, and getting enough exercise. Doctors today are concerned about the number of children who spend too much time in front of the television or playing computer games. For good health, children need plenty of sunshine, fresh air, and outside activity.

Good health habits include eating well-balanced meals. Most parents in the United States are aware of what their children should be eating. Some children, however, resist eating what is on their plate. These children don't realize that the cells in our bodies need certain vitamins and minerals to fight off infection and disease. Unless these children take vitamin pills every day, they will certainly suffer from diseases or illnesses caused by vitamin deficiency.

Other good health habits, such as washing your hands frequently and brushing your teeth, are essential to stay well.

Many people say that you can't buy good health. What that means is that you can have all the money in the world, but if you don't take good care of yourself, and practice good health habits daily, you will not be healthy. It is much better to prevent health problems than to treat them with medicine and doctor visits.

If you practice good health habits, and keep your immune system strong, you should stay well and resist becoming sick.

God gave you a body to use for a lifetime. In today's world, most healthy people are living into their eighties. Many people are grandparents and even great-grandparents. If you take care of yourself and keep healthy while you are young, you are less likely to have health problems when you become older.

 Practical Application: How good is your resistance?

There are many good health habits that help to strengthen your immune system and resistance to germs and diseases. Following are some questions that will help you to know which ones you already practice, and which ones you need to improve.

1. Do you sleep about eight to ten hours every night? _____

2. Do you eat health-building foods each day, especially fruits and vegetables? _____ Which ones? _____

3. Do you get enough daily exercise, walking, running and playing outdoors in fresh air and sunshine? _____ How much? _____

4. Do you participate in sports? _____ Which ones? _____ _____

5. Do you drink enough water especially on hot days? _____ How much? _____

6. Do you wear clothing that keeps your body and head warm and dry in cold weather? _____

7. Do you visit your doctor and dentist regularly for check ups? ____

8. Do you brush and floss your teeth at least two times a day? _____

9. Do you wash your hands before you eat and after you use the bathroom? _____

10. Do you stay away from people who have an infectious disease? _____

11. Are you careful to use clean glasses, cups, dishes, and silverware? _____

12. Do you pray daily for good health for you and your family? _____

If you answered "yes" to these questions, you are practicing good health habits that strengthen your immune system and keep your resistance to disease at a high level. If not, it is time to make some improvements in your daily health habits.

Make a list of five good health habits you would like to follow to improve your health:

1. _____

2. _____

3. _____

4. _____

5. _____

Resisting disease, however, is not our only battle in life. We must also resist the temptation to stray from God's commandments by keeping ourselves spiritually healthy. Scripture instructs us as to what we should do to protect our spiritual health and strength, as in Ephesians 6:13-17 below.

"Put on the armor of God, that you may be able to resist on the evil day and, having done everything, to hold your ground. So stand strong with your waist belted in truth, clothed in goodness as a breastplate, and your feet shod in readiness for the gospel of peace. In all situations, hold faith as a shield, to stop all the flaming arrows of the evil one. And take the helmet of salvation and the sword of the Spirit, which is the Word of God."

C. The Family Doctor

We usually think of a doctor as the person we go to when we are sick to help us get well. However, we don't go to doctors only when we are sick. We go to the doctor for regular checkups so he can help us to stay well. Your mother has probably already taken you to your family doctor for well-person checkups and to give you help to protect you from illnesses. Your mother and father know what is best for you.

Vaccines are now available. A vaccine is a substance that contains a weakened type of germ which causes the body to produce antibodies that prevent a person from getting a disease caused by that germ. We call this an immunization. With a vaccine, a person becomes "immune" to that disease. While many vaccines have been proven over the years, when new vaccines come on the market, parents must decide what is best for their children.

The first vaccine was developed by Dr. Edward Jenner over two hundred years ago. It was a smallpox vaccine. Today, we have vaccines that protect us against diphtheria, whooping cough, measles, tetanus, and polio. Many parents ask doctors to give their young children most of these vaccines. Later, the children receive booster shots or doses that keep them immune or safe from these diseases.

Before vaccines were discovered, many children died of infectious diseases. Polio was especially harmful. It not only killed some children, but crippled many more. Some years ago, Dr. Jonas Salk and Dr. Albert Sabin were successful in making vaccines to protect children from polio.

Remember that your mother and father are the best judges of what is good for you. God has given them the graces to make decisions about your health and the health of your family.

D. Wonder Drugs

There are times when some germs can make you very sick and you are having a hard time getting well on your own. At those times, your mother may take you to see a doctor who may give you one of the germ killing drugs. We call these drugs wonder drugs because they work wondrously fast to make you well by stopping the growth of germs.

One group of drugs is known as the sulfa drugs. Another group of drugs is called antibiotics (an' ti bi ot' iks). The discovery of these two groups of drugs has saved the lives of millions of people. The sulfa drugs and antibiotics kill germs by preventing their growth.

In the past, people died in their thirties and forties. Most soldiers died from their wounds. God has blessed the work of doctors and research scientists so that today, people are living and even working into their seventies and eighties.

You should never take any medicine, however, unless it is given to you by your mother or father. Parents are given special graces by God to raise their children. Drugs can be dangerous if they are taken by the wrong people at the wrong times.

 Review Exercise IV.

1. What does **resistance** mean when people use it in talking about disease and health? _____

2. What is a **vaccine?** _____
    _____

3. List several diseases for which there are vaccines. _____
    _____

4. What disease was a special threat to children before a vaccine was discovered?
    _____

5. How do sulfa drugs and antibiotics work? _____
    _____

6. Who is in charge of giving you medicine? _____

7. What did God give your parents to help them make decisions about the health for you and your family? _____

Review for Chapter 8
Safety & Health

Health Words I.

In each space below, choose the word that fits best with each word meaning given. Choose from these words:

poison   first aid   bruise   bandage   gauze   sterile.

1. _____ a strip of cloth or other material used to cover a cut

2. _____ a wound caused by a fall or blow that makes the skin change color

3. _____ a strip of material that can be used in making a bandage

4. _____ free from germs

5. _____ the first help given to accident victims

Health Ideas I.

In the spaces provided, write **T** for True statements, and **F** for False statements.

1. ____ A bruise should be bathed in hot water.

2. ____ All burns should be treated by a doctor.

3. ____ A good treatment for a small cut is to wash it with soap and water.

4. ____ A cut should be kept clean.

5. ____ Someone else's medicine can never harm you.

Health Rules I.

Directions: Write **F** for each rule that tells how to prevent falls; **B** for each rule that tells how to prevent burns; and **C** for each rule that tells how to prevent cuts.

1. ____ Stay away from boards with nails.

2. ____ Keep the points of sharp objects down when you hand them to others.

3. ____ Avoid standing or sitting close to a fire.

4. ____ Climb only on things built for climbing.

5. ____ Never run while carrying a pointed object.

6. ____ Always keep your shoelaces tied.

7. ____ Hold sharp objects with the tips pointed toward the floor.

8. ____ Stay away from worn wires.

9. ____ Use a strong and stable ladder when you want to reach something up high.

10. ____ When climbing, hold on with both hands.

Health Rules II.

Directions: Put a check mark by each sentence below which indicates a good health rule that you should follow.

1. ____ Wash your hands before you eat.

2. ____ Wash your hands after using the bathroom.

3. ____ Use dental floss at least once a day.

4. ____ Try to stay away from other people when you have a cold.

5. ____ Don't put dirty things in your mouth, like pencils or pens.

Health Rules III.

Directions: Complete the following health rules by choosing one of the words below.

    noise   *strike*   *swallow*   *infection*   *listen*   *wax*

1. When coming down in an elevator, _____ several times.

2. Open your mouth when you expect a loud _____.

3. Be careful not to _____ anyone on the ear.

4. The first sign of an _____ in your middle ear is an earache.

5. Only a skilled person should remove _____ from your ears.

Health Words II.

Directions: Write the following words next to the correct statement.

    a) vaccine   b) immune   c) antibodies   d) antibiotics
    e) deficiency   f) bacteria   g) cavities   h) germs

1. Drugs that keep some germs from growing inside the body are called

    _____.

2. Organisms so small that they can be seen only under a microscope are

    named _____.

3. A substance containing a weakened or dead germ is called a

    _____.

4. Bacteria in your mouth can cause _____ in your teeth.

5. When you are protected from a particular disease, you are said to be

    _____.

6. Diseases such as scarlet fever and tuberculosis are caused by _____.

7. Substances that the body sends into the blood to fight germs are called

    _____.

8. Lack of something that the body needs for good health is a _____.

Health Ideas II.

Directions: Circle the word or words that make each sentence true.

1. Milk is made safe to drink by (vaccination, pasteurization).

2. (Antibodies, Bacteria) are very tiny organisms that help plants to grow.

3. Among the diseases caused by viruses are polio, chicken pox, and (tuberculosis, colds).

4. (Bacteria, Viruses) increase in number by dividing in two when they reach full size.

5. A person who is strong and healthy is said to have good (organs, immunity, blood).

6. There are (white, red) cells in the blood that are able to surround germs and kill them.

7. (Parents, Children) should decide about medicines.

Health Rules IV.

Directions: Write Yes or No for each statement that gives a good health rule to follow.

1. _____ Put something cold on a bruise.

2. _____ Have a dentist examine and clean your teeth regularly.

3. _____ Stay away from someone who is coughing.

4. _____ Your parents should decide about the medicine to protect you against disease.

5. _____ Never drink water unless you are sure that it is safe.

6. _____ Pay no attention to a cold unless your body temperature is above normal.

7. _____ Brush your teeth after meals.

GLOSSARY

Andes – mountain system in South America

Andromeda – a constellation

antennae – the long slender paired segment sensory organs on the head of an insect

antibiotics – substance produced by or derived by chemical alteration of a substance produced by a microorganism that kills another microorganism

antibody – a substance produced by the body that counteracts the effects of a disease germ or its poisons

antiseptic – a substance that kills germs or makes them harmless, such as iodine or hydrogen peroxide.

asteroids – large rocky bodies that wander between the planets, also called minor planets

astronaut – a traveler in a spacecraft

atmosphere – layer of air around the earth which extends about 100 miles out from the surface

basalt – a dark fine-grained igneous rock

Big Dipper – the constellation which resembles a large water dipper

carbon dioxide – heavy colorless gas found in earth's atmosphere produced by exhaling of humans and animals

Cassiopeia – a constellation named after a mythical queen of Ethiopia and mother of Andromeda; the constellation is found between Andromeda and Cepheus

cell – the basic unit of which all plants and animals are made up.

comet – a small bright celestial body that developed a long tail when near the sun

compass – a device for determining direction by means of a magnetic needle swinging freely and pointing to the magnetic north

constellation – any of 88 groups of stars forming patterns thought of as figures or designs

contagious – transmitted by contact with an infected person

crater – depression formed by the impact of a meteorite

diphtheria – contagious bacterial disease marked by fever and by coating of the air passages with a membrane that interferes with breathing

Earth – the fifth largest planet in the solar system, and the only planet known to sustain life

eclipse – a complete or partial hiding of the sun caused by the moon's passing between the sun and the earth

electric current – a movement of positive or negative electric particles

electrical appliances – machines that run by the movement of electricity through them

ellipse – a closed curve of oval shape

equator – an imaginary circle around the earth that is everywhere equally distant from the two poles

eruption – material erupted by a volcano, marked by lava (molten rock) spewing from the earth

force – an influence (as a push or a pull) that causes motion or a change of motion

frictional force – the force that resists motion between bodies in contact

fungus – any of a large group of plantlike organisms (mushrooms, molds, and yeasts) that have no chlorophyll and live on other plants or animals or on decaying materials

germ – a microbe that causes disease

granite – a hard granular igneous rock used especially for buildings and monuments.

gravity – the gravitational attraction (force) or the mass of a celestial object (as earth) for bodies close to it

hydroelectric dam – a dam employed in the production of electricity by waterpower

immunity – the natural power of the body to resist infection

limestone – rock that is formed by accumulation of organic remains, used in building

Mediterranean Sea – a land-locked sea located between Europe and Africa

metamorphosis – a sudden and very great change in appearance or structure, such as of a caterpillar into a butterfly

microbes – germs

molecule – the smallest particle of matter that is the same chemically as the whole mass

nebula – any of numerous clouds of gas or dust in interstellar space

nerves – strands of nervous tissue that carry nerve impulses between the brain and spinal cord and every part of the body

nitrogen/oxygen – the gases which make up most of the earth's atmosphere; oxygen is necessary for living things to breathe

Nobel Prize – any of various annual prizes established by the will of Alfred Nobel for the encouragement of persons who work for the interests of humanity

nutrition – the processes by which a living being takes in and uses nutrients

orbit – a path described by one body in its revolution about another

organism – a living thing having parts and functioning as a whole

paramecium – any of a genus of slipper shaped protozoans that move by cilia

pasteurization – a process of preserving beverages such as milk or beer by heating them at a temperature high enough to kill many harmful germs and then cooling it rapidly

phosphorus – a nonmetallic chemical element that has characteristics similar to nitrogen

physiology – a branch of biology dealing with the functions and functioning of living matter and organisms

planet – any of the large bodies in the solar system that revolve around the sun

plant – a living thing with cellulose cell walls, without sense organs, and without ability to move about (grasses, trees, seaweeds, and fungi).

polio – a virus disease marked by inflammation of the nerve cells of the spinal cord

pollination – in flowers, the process of fertilization by transferring pollen from an anther to the stigma for reproduction

polonium – a radioactive metallic chemical element, named for the birthplace of its discoverer Marie Curie

purified – free from impurities or noxious matter

radium – a very radioactive metallic chemical element that is used in the treatment of cancer

rickets – a childhood deficiency disease marked especially by soft deformed bones and caused by inadequate sunlight or inadequate Vitamin D

rocket – a jet engine that operates on the same principle as a firework rocket but carries the oxygen needed for burning its fuel

Rockies – mountain system in western North America

root hairs – the many hairlike tubular outgrowths of the tap root

rotation – the act of turning about an axis or a center

scarlet fever – a contagious disease marked by fever, sore throat, and red rash and caused by certain streptococci

scurvy – a deficiency disease marked by bleeding gums, loosened teeth, and bleeding under the skin; caused by a lack of Vitamin C

sulfa – any of various synthetic organic bacteria–inhibiting drugs

tendons – a tough cord of dense white fibrous tissue uniting muscle with another part (such as a bone)

thermal expansion – increase in linear dimensions of a solid or in volume of a fluid because of rise in temperature

tuberculosis – a communicable bacterial disease typically marked by wasting, fever, and formation of cheesy tubercles often in the lungs

turbo prop engine – a jet engine having a turbine propeller and designed to produce thrust principally by means of a propeller, although additional thrust is usually obtained from the hot exhaust gases which issue in a jet

typhoid fever – a communicable bacterial disease marked by fever, diarrhea, prostration, and intestinal inflammation

universe – all created things including the earth and celestial bodies viewed as making up one system

ultraviolet rays – having a wavelength shorter than those of visible light and longer than those of x-rays

vaccine – a substance containing weakened germs to cause your body to produce antibodies against a disease, usually administered by injection

whooping cough – an infectious bacterial disease—especially of children— marked by convulsive coughing fits often followed by a shrill gasping intake of breath

NOTES

NOTES

NOTES

NOTES

NOTES

NOTES

NOTES

NOTES

NOTES

NOTES

NOTES

NOTES